1

Table of Contents

INTRODUCTION

Cricut is the newest of a selection of private digital cutting machines specializing in die cutting items for home decoration, scrapbooking, paper cutting, card making, and much more. Everything you can do using a Cricut is only restricted by your creativity. These machines include Cricut cartridges for simple use. The cartridges consist of numerous amazing built-in templates for a variety of functions and dimensions.

This device is also very simple to take care of. The layouts can be selected from the cartridge or can be custom manufactured using the Cricut design studio to take your imagination to higher heights - but a computer is needed for this objective.

The Cricut package includes the following:

- Cricut machines: These are the resources which perform the real cutting because of your creative layouts.
- Gypsy: This is actually the total Cricut cartridge library at one go. It's a hand-held apparatus that features the entire Cricut design studio - so anytime we need to operate on a layout, the gypsy is conveniently available.
- Cricut Design Studio: It's the full-fledged program for creating any layout on a Cricut cutter. All you will need is a PC. One disappointment to your clients is the Cricut Design Studio isn't mac compatible. In addition, it can be

used to readily Explore, cut and layout the whole cartridge library. The program also offers a choice to save the layout for future demands. Assessing a Cricut layout has never been simpler!

- Cuttlebug: It's the private die cutting and embossing system. It comprises various sizes and styles such as paper-crafting, home decoration, house jobs, events, and college projects. The plan is produced by top artists and provides sharp die cuts each and every time. Cuttlebug also includes professional excellent embossing for connections using its different feel and measurements, which makes it an amazing system.

- Cricut cake: This is an optional piece of equipment used for creating designer confectioneries for cakes and other treats, in virtually no time.

- Cricut Expression: This is an advanced version that may be used for sheets as large as 24" x 12", so it can fit any aspect, be it professional or personal. Additionally, it boasts of several cartridges and innovative options, such as the adding of colours, printing, and much more, which makes it perfect for many projects.

Cricut is the handicraft enthusiast's best friend, or for anybody who likes to design and create. It provides over 250 different designs in various sizes. The layouts could be smaller than an inch or bigger up to one inch. The 8 different cutting angles provide precision reduction - all this together with appealing templates and stylized alphabets, offers much to pick from.

Before you buy your very first Cricut, it is important to consider all probable options to decide on the very best machine to match your crafting needs.

First, you must stock up on the fundamentals, such as Cricut ribbon and picture cartridges. These cartridges come in a variety of topics to showcase and commemorate any event, like vacations or forthcoming events. You'll also need a large quantity of coloured paper, along with a pad on which to cut that contrasts to the dimensions of your system.

If you are an avid scrapbooker, you ought to start looking into buying your first Cricut cutter or the Cricut Expression. This system will cut shapes, letters and themes to decorate your scrapbook pages. It is also possible to decorate bulletin boards, posters, party decorations, greeting cards or invitations of any sort. These cutters can also cut cloth. It's encouraged for you to starch the cloth first so as to make the job as simple as possible for your own system to finish. The gap between both is straightforward.

The Cricut Expression is a brand new, 12" x 24" version of the first Cricut. This system makes it easier to create large-scale jobs in a massive quantity – as long as you've got the right quantity of paper. Font and picture cartridges may be utilised in the two machines.

Have you heard of the Cricut Cake? This useful cutter is designed to cut nearly anything for baked products, such as frosting sheets, gum paste, fondant, cookie dough, tortillas, baking soda, gum and the majority of other soft food substances. Whatever material you choose to use must be between 1/6" and 1/8" thick. Keep the blade clean at all times so as to make sure you get the very best cut possible.

Another favourite Cricut option is the Cricut Cuttlebug. This system is small. It merely cuts paper that's 6 inches wide and weighs just 7 lbs. The Cuttlebug is mainly used for cutting and embossing specific crafts. This is the best way to decorate several greeting card type invitations. Once you include a range of coloured dies, the Cuttlebug is ready to emboss straight away. These dies are also harmonious with Sizzix, Big Shot and Thin Cuts machines, which serve a similar function.

Are you currently curious and are creating your personal t-shirts and cloth designs? Cricut also created the Yudu for all those crafters who love screen-printing and producing their own layouts. The Yudu enables its owners to attach it to a laser ink jet printer and make a layout to screen-print onto virtually anything!

Yudus are used for straps, handbags, photograph frames, shoes - you name it.

Finally, if you would like to feed your newfound Cricut obsession, go right ahead and buy one of the newest Cricut Gypsys. This useful, hand-held apparatus will keep your font cartridges ready for simple portable use. It's possible to design from anyplace on the move, in the physician's office, even while on holiday, or merely sitting on your sofa. Anything you plan on the Gypsy is totally transferable to a Cricut device for die cutting. If you save your layout, it may be linked to one of your Cricut apparatus and published at a later moment.

This is a short overview of some of the cutting-edge machines Cricut sells. As you can see there's a fantastic assortment of machines for whichever specific kind of craft you wish to concentrate on. One thing is for certain. Whichever machine you select you will have many hours of inspiration and fun producing and creating your own crafting projects.

Cricut is your go-to brand for a selection of private digital cutting machines specializing in die cutting of items for home decoration, scrapbooking, paper cutting, card making, and much more. Everything you can do using a Cricut is only restricted by your creativity.

Complex Cricut suggestions for the craft project

Cricut private cutters are carrying handcrafts to a whole new level. People throughout the country are astonished at the amazing and advanced Cricut thoughts this machine may bring to your job listing. You can create almost anything amazing and one of a kind working with the Cricut cartridges.

How does a Cricut machine function? It is very straightforward. Simply load a Cricut cartridge to the machine, choose what colour card stock you would like to use for your individual layout and cut off. Each cartridge has different themed layouts from seasonal layouts to favourite cartoon characters. You can pick from the cut-out layouts to use for scrapbooks, picture frames, customized greeting cards, wall hangings, calendars and a lot more.

One of the amazing Cricut ideas it is possible to create as a craft is the Cricut calendar. Every month can be produced in another page and you'll be able to decorate these pages using various layouts. Wouldn't it be wonderful to make your February page employing the Love-struck Season cartridge? The Easter cartridge will supply you with endless layouts for the April page of the calendar. Your May calendar could be made with the Mother's Day cartridge. How interesting would it be to style your July page with trimmings made with the Independence Day season cartridge? December can be outfitted together with All the

Joys of the Season cartridge and the Snow Friend's cartridge. You may select items to your heart's content.

Another fantastic idea you may make is a scrapbook. This well-loved craft job is why Cricut cutting machine were devised in the first place. Together with the Cricut die cutting machine, you can personalize scrapbooks for your kids, for mother-daughter or dad and son keepsakes. Cricut created cartridges that each little child would delight in using like the Once Upon a Princess cartridge or the Disney Tinker Bell and Friends' cartridge. Your small superhero would certainly love the Batman layout in the Batman: The Brave and the Bold or Robots cartridges. Cricut provides you lots of layouts to select from for scrapbooking ideas.

The Cricut layouts aren't only layout ideas, but additionally have fonts and alphabets in the Sesame Street font cartridge along with the Ashlyn's alphabet cartridge. Use these exciting tools when making your personalized gift like a wall-hanging picture frame for framing a photograph of an unforgettable occasion of the receiver of your gift. Embellish your wall hanging with pretty cut-outs produced by the Cricut cutter.

Your Cricut ideas are endless by means of this superb machine and also the Cricut cartridges to suit any event and job possible to consider. Creating a Cricut job with the entire family is a superb way to spend some time together and producing those gorgeous items can be a superb experience for everyone to achieve.

Ideas that could generate income

People really feel the Cricut machine is the one instrument that's responsible for the conceptualization of those layouts which we see in scrapbooks. In fact, the designs are derived in the brain of the consumer and are made concrete by the Cricut cutting machine.

In addition, there are other tools which help create the layouts such as cartridges and applications tools. The top software tool out there's is the Cricut Design Studio. With this application, you can create and edit your own designs and also edit current designs which are pre-packed.

Life is great indeed! People also believe the use of a Cricut cutting system is only restricted to the area of scrapbooking. Only a few men and women may know, but the Cricut machine in addition to the cartridges and the software tools may be used for a large number of things. There are a whole lot of Cricut projects which it is possible to use the Cricut cutting system for and only your mind can restrict what you could do.

Greeting cards are excellent Cricut projects for everyone to participate in. Together with the layouts you may receive from the

Cricut cartridge along with the software tools you have set up; you can lay out covers that withstand the unconventional. The difficulty most men and women experience when they attempt to buy greeting cards is they can't find the type of card they're searching for. This may result in stress and a great deal of frustration on the purchaser's part. You're so much better off making your own personal greeting cards.

Cricut calendars are another fantastic reason to get a Cricut cutting device. A calendar is full of 12 months. You can get creative and search for layouts on your cartridge or software which could reflect the month that's inside your calendar. If we're at the month of December, then you can search for layouts that fit the mood and feeling of December. Start looking for snowmen, reindeers, and Christmas trees. I promise you that you have all of the layouts you will ever desire inside of your own software or cartridge.

Keep in mind, only your imagination can restrict what you do. These Cricut projects may be used either for individual satisfaction or revenue generating functions. Be imaginative with your Cricut machine. You never know what crazy thoughts can pop into your mind.

From the universe of record making, an individual may believe there are only hardware resources such as the Cricut cutting machine, as well as the Cricut Expression system. But there also are software tools which may help you create great Cricut ideas that could help you in the creation of your perfect scrapbook.

One of them is your Cricut Design Studio. This software tool is a fresh method for connecting your initial machine to your own computer and it may also works with the Cricut Expression. With the usage of an onscreen cutting mat, this program tool allows Explore, layout, and cutting from the whole Cricut cartridge library. The excellent thing about this is what you see is what you cut! Additionally, this application has an interface which is extremely user - friendly and has the capacity to store any of your own creations. This is a tool which any scrapbooker should get!

With this tool, it is possible to do anything and create countless Cricut ideas. The general rule here is to allow your creativity to know no limitations. When you make a scrapbook, the most important objective is to make layouts that jive with all the images you set in. Let us say for instance, you add some pictures of your wedding day.

You need to select or create a layout that will make an impression that could make anybody who looks at the images and the scrapbooks relive the memories. The exact same general rule will apply to anybody. You might even generate income out of this by helping people develop designs for their scrapbook.

The usage of the computer software isn't confined to only creating scrapbooks. As stated, earlier, let your creativity set the limitations and there should be no limitations. Besides scrapbooks, the next things you can make include: a. Wall hangings b. Image frames c. Greeting cards

Maybe the most frequent innovation of the Cricut machine aside from scrapbooks is Cricut calendars. The layouts which you receive from a Cricut system may be used to include spice and life to any calendar. With the usage of a Cricut machine in addition to the software applications, you may produce layouts for every month in a calendar year. The trick is to pick any layout that could reflect exactly what that particular month is all about. October for instance where the very best layout is always a backdrop depicting Oktoberfest.

So, there you've got it, a few excellent Cricut ideas which could help you make money or just simply make you happier. Bear in mind, it's your own choice. Get ready to have a rocking good time!

Cricut cartridges are mainly the core of a Cricut cutting machine, which can be put within the cutter system to turn the layout just as the consumer wishes into a bit of paper.

A broad variety of cartridges can be found on the market, although not all these cartridges operate with all sorts of machines. As an example, the Cricut cartridge operates with Cricut machines only, and it's the vital element whereby crafters and artists can create many designs in wonderful colours and styles.

Together with the changes in printing technologies, a selection of cartridges was introduced recently with more packages to pick from compared to prior ones. The two main kinds of printer cartridges available are: the ink (used with an ink-jet printer), and laser cartridges, used in laser printers. In the case of all Cricut machines, they still use ink-jet printers easily.

All about Cricut ink cartridges:
At first, Cricut ink cartridges were only available in black, but after some time, a few different colours were introduced. Afterwards, together with advancements in printing technology, ink cartridges have been developed, and attempts were made to present different font styles, layout and colours for forming contours, too.

The key to the success of the Cricut system, is the use of distinct and special kinds of cartridges that enable users to obtain, cut and create in almost any font, layout, colour and design.

The general types of Cricut cartridges are:

* **Font cartridge:** It includes full alphabets, numbers and other symbols together with font styles and other font organizing shapes. Some of the favourite all-year seasonal and around cartridges comprise Forever Young, Jasmine, Teardrop, Lyrical Letters, Pumpkin carving for Halloween, Thanksgiving holiday, Winter Wonderland for the Christmas season, etc.

* **Shape cartridge:** It includes an assortment of shapes including boxes, tags, bags, animals, sports, paper dolls, etc.

* **Licensed cartridge**: It enables users to find the cut designed with favourite figures such as Disney's Micky Mouse, Hello Kitty, Pixar's Toy Story, etc.

* **Classmate cartridge**: As its name implies, is made specifically for classroom functions, which includes classroom fonts, shapes and classroom layout, visual analysis program, suggestions and representations of educators, etc.

* **Solutions cartridge**: It costs less than the rest. The shapes include welding, baseball, soccer, campout, etc.

The wide variety of Cricut cartridges, as mentioned above, provides crafters, particularly young customers, an opportunity to experiment with their artistic skills without the support of a computer, whereas the Cricut ink cartridge makes it a lot easier for them to create designs in a variety of shapes and colours.

CHAPTER 1

WHAT IS CRICUT DESIGN?

You have a Cricut cutting machine (the original Cricut, Cricut Expression, or even Cricut Create). After playing with it for a while, and even squandering a lot of paper with your errors, you know there's yet another item in the market called Cricut Design Studio. The Cricut Design studio software lets you learn what you are very likely to cut on your Cricut cutter before you cut the paper. It lets you connect letters together, alter shapes, etc.

The Cricut Design Studio program enables you to view before you cut, which is really a substantial paper saver. So, you should break down and purchase the Cricut Design Studio program. You start it up and there's a program disc, and a user guide about the very best way to set up the program along with a few basic conditions and applications, a USB cable plus a cunning mouse pad that is configured. You load the app onto your own computer and following that in the event that you are like me you say "what the hell do I do now?"

Cricut design studio from Provo Craft

Many crafting lovers have fallen in love with their die cutting system, "the Cricut." A brand-new addition to this popular product is the growth of a software program created just for Cricut users.

If you maybe you've found a passion for the Provo Craft Cricut cutting machines, then you are very likely to fall in love all over again as soon as you try the latest accession to the Cricut home - Cricut design studio program.

Cricut Design Studio is a computer program application produced by Provo Craft, the makers of the Cricut machine. Although the system itself empowers the user to cut unique fonts and shapes in a rage of measurements, the Cricut Design Studio takes it into an entirely new level. Simply connect the Cricut to the computer with a USB port, install the program, and unleash a totally new measurement of crafting.

The Cricut design studio gives an entirely new dimension to your Cricut adventures, if you have the very first small Cricut or perhaps the larger Cricut Expression. One of the best components is this app is easy to use and understand. It's not vital to become a computer whiz to find it out and you may conduct an excellent number of imaginative effects together with the addition of this 1 slice of software.

The principal benefit of the Cricut Design Studio is your capacity for customers to weld, or perhaps link letters together with one another to form a single cutting edge. Gone are the cases of having to copy each letter at a time. Now letters, phrases, words and shapes can be plotted together before cutting making it faster and simpler than ever to add cuttings to jobs.

Another advantage of the Cricut Design Studio consists of that the shapes and letters that can be manipulated extensively before cutting. Users aren't restricted to only adjusting the measurements but may now change the shape attributes to better support their overall design. Each image may be elongated, reversed and made invisible to discover the particular look the crafter currently needs.

Even though the Cricut design studio includes benefit after benefit, my own personal favourite is the capability to incorporate pictures from a number of cartridges into one design. The user can design together with the cartridge options concurrently instead of being limited to cutting using one cartridge at a time.

Advanced along with ultra-creative users have created lots inspiring ideas by mixing many different cartridges to create unbelievable cutting-edge designs.

The Cricut Design Studio can also be in my own estimation, a necessity for each and every Cricut owner. Though there's a learning curve for it, after it is understood the creative options are totally infinite. The Cricut in addition to all the Design Studio has become a must-have resource for every scrapbooker and card maker today.

Here are just a few items that have helped me with all of the Cricut Design Studio software, and it will help you.

1. Loaded within this Cricut Design Studio software package is accessibility to all or any cartridges. Another wonderful element of this application is that with every new cartridge that is easily available that you purchase, you might just get on the Internet and update your software to the latest edition. Considering the Cricut Design Studio app has all the current cartridges, you are going to be able to list those that you need and then purchase them or put them on your want list. Notice: You are going to be able to use each cartridge that is in the Cricut Design Studio software, however you need to find that cartridge packaged in your Cricut cutter to actually use the image.

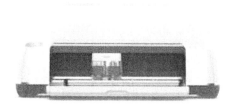

2. The manual describes welding. Welding is connecting letters or graphics together. Just remember if you want to combine it, you will need to look at the box to get the information onto your screen. The welding feature is excellent if analysing phrases or words. It will create the tradition of sticking it to your scrapbook page or greeting card super easy. When trimming letters that aren't welded together, you need to be cautious they're implemented directly as well as the spacing is good.

3. The Cricut Design studio app even has a feature that lets you use quite a few cartridges whenever you are creating a layout. For example: you're creating a birthday card that reads Happy Birthday Tapioca. You choose to use the tear drop cartridge for the words Happy Birthday and you would love to use the Jasmine cartridge to make the word Tapioca. This really isn't any trouble with this particular Cricut Design Studio program. The moment your Cricut is cutting it's likely to allow you to understand just what cartridge to load into your own Cricut cutter. How cool is that? The Cricut Design Studio program even allows you to create anything your imagination will allow. There are unlimited possibilities for your creativeness employing the Cricut Design Studio program.

WHY GET THE DESIGN STUDIO?

The Cricut Design Studio lets you combine images from a number of these cartridges you have and unite them into one design. It's possible to arrange your design before you set it to a cartridge. It's very easy to weld letters together, shrink or expand pictures, set a photo on a diagonal, and then stretch, rotate, or even use other images. You might even stop and save your design before it's completed, then return to finish it. At any time, you have the design just the way you want it, just slide in the first cartridge needed and push 1 button. The moment your Cricut reaches the stage where it needs another cartridge, then it will alert you so you might swap the cartridges. When you finish, it is possible to save your design into your computer or flash drive and you'll be able to share it with your friends.

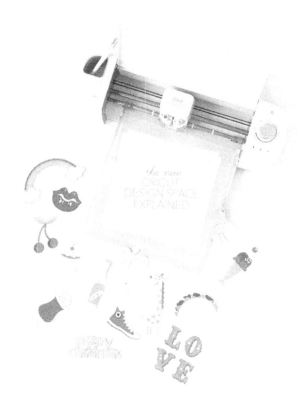

Another benefit of Design Studio is it is possible to test every available design in the complete Cricut library, even if you've got the cartridge or not. Simply type in keywords to search for a particular image or word and you are in a position to determine exactly how it might look in your own ideas. This can let you decide on whether you'd like to get a particular cartridge or not. You could also preplant your design and save it until you get the crucial cartridge or borrow it from a friend.

Are there cons to the Cricut Design Studio?

The sole con is that you are restricted to using Design Studio at a spot where you've got access to a computer. In the event you've got a laptop, however, that is a non-issue.

In general, the Cricut Design Studio is a great addition to a Cricut collection. You are only limited by your own creativity.

One of the terrific benefits of possessing Cricut Design Studio is your capability to collaborate with others. Everyone who designs something can save it on their computer. Many elect to put the file online and allow other individuals to use their designs. The moment you get started browsing other people's work, you're going to be amazed at the incredible work of these generous and talented Cricut users. Following is a step-by-step manual to downloading and cutting along with other people's files.

You will discover different websites and sites that have work posted together with the design archives. Every person can shop and share their designs in a different way. Many use a third-party sharing site, although others keep the files hosted right there on their website. A range of the files on the Cricut.com message panel are saved as a text document and need to be changed before using them.

After you've discovered a file you want to use, you can begin the download process.

1. Click the link they have provided for you to the file. When it is hosted on their website, it will ask you if you'd love to begin, cancel or save. In the event the file is hosted on a file sharing site it will let you wait for the to "click here to download file." When you select that link it will take you into the display that asks if you want to begin, save or cancel.

2. Once you're on the open or shop display, you are going to need to choose save. Before you do it, make sure the file is showing the place where you want the file to be saved. You may opt to make a folder specifically for Cricut documents. If you'd like to change the document name, then take action at this phase. Click here to begin saving the file to your PC.

Now the file is on your computer, it's likely to start it within the Cricut Design Studio application. Stick to these easy activities to cut a layout that is stored.

1. Open the Cricut Design Studio app. Look on the "file" drop down menu in the top left corner and then choose "available."

2. After selecting "open" a screen will develop that shows cut files that were saved in the "my tasks" folder. These are files of your own you have made. To find the file that was downloaded and saved, find the folder where you saved it by picking it in the "look in" region.

3. Pick the document you will need to begin and click on the open button. This will bring up the file you downloaded and open it on your personal computer. To cut it, load the paper then click the scissors to cut it off. You might can also alter or boost the document in the event you need to, but be sure to always give credit where credit is expected instead of keeping a design as your own unless you created the entire file.

Spend some time browsing other people's designs and work and you will soon have more ideas and files than you can cut. Make sure you leave an opinion or a thank you after you use someone else's files and discuss exactly what you've created if at all possible. Start searching for an approaching article to show how to obtain files from the Cricut message boards and alter them in text files to create documents.

When you open your Cricut layout studio software, you will see 4 main elements: the electronic mat where your job is displayed, the Cricut cartridge library, the electronic key-pad overlay and the shape properties window.

The library includes posts of every Cricut cartridge printed. As more come out, you'll be able to improve your library so you can always get new tools into your creations. You're absolutely free to design with the cartridges in the plan studio library nonetheless, it's possible to simply cut using just the cartridges you have. The library can be used to provide you study content from the cartridges that you do not have, therefore use it like a tool that is going to support you to find precisely what you adore!

Searching through the library is straightforward. The Cricut cartridge library permits you to list a cartridge location in whatever arrangement you choose in the drop-down menu. You can organize your library list alphabetically by favourites by category or by the cartridges you have. It's also possible to browse through the library by using keywords (Tip: if you do a search by keyword, the simpler the search term, the greater!) Together with the auto-filler function anticipates what you might be looking for and provides you tips.

As you cycle during your Explore results, the electronic overlay alterations to show that cartridge location and feature your search outcome is situated in. This process makes it a whole lot simpler to get precisely what you want quickly. You can even customize exactly what screens in the electronic overlay if you happen to decide what it shows for your keyword isn't accurate.

The key-pad overlay is all but identical with the actual overlays that you set on your Cricut device. On the rear, you'll find the six feature buttons, both the "shift-lock" button, and the space/backspace buttons. Following the shift-lock buttons are engaged, they are highlighted like on the Cricut apparatus. When you set your mouse pointer on your image keys, then they are going to expand marginally to reveal the image key you will pick.

Working together with the virtual mat is just as natural as it gets. When you have chosen the contour which you want to use, it will appear on the electronic mat jointly with choice of controls. Selection choices are the 8 bands that show regarding the corners and sides of this shape. Virtually all of your image crafting will be carried out with these choices, as you execute them you will see the possibilities available to your creative ideas.

Welding basics

One of the easiest things you're likely to need to perform with the Cricut Design Studio is to put letters together to type a phrase. There are two approaches to link letters together. The first is to work along with the expression as one picture that may be manipulated together. The following method will be to make every individual letter as one picture that can be manipulated independently.

As you sort the letters into your own word, you will see they show up on the outside mat shortly one after another. When you decide on the pair of letters by clicking on a few of these lines, any alterations such as size will be applied to every one of those letters at the same time. Another strategy is to produce one letter, then hit enter prior to scanning the following. This creates each letter separately so you may control each letter individually.

To weld a word when the letters are just one group, adhere to the following steps:
Click on the word using the mouse so it is chosen.
Kerning is the space between letters. Put this in -.005 or leave at no cost. Reach applies.
The letters will go collectively, some may be touching while others may not. Decide on every letter in the word. It'll become a hurried line when that particular letter is selected. Transfer it together with all the nudge arrows until each connection is somewhat overlapping.
Opt for the whole word again and again analyze the welding box under shape properties.

The phrase will likely have dark lines showing where the clipping will be, whereas a lighter line will probably indicate where it has been welded together.

You will find times when you are going to need to use every single letter or graphic individually. This is quite helpful when you may need one letter dimension and then another letter or another dimension. To weld letters that are individual, follow these measures:

Pick the very first letter you're likely to need to use. Be sure to hit to deselect the connection prior to adding a new one.

Opt for another letter you will use. Notice that if you decide on each letter, it is its own letter. It could possibly be manipulated and not affect others at all.

Continue integrating letters and be sure to hit enter after each.

In this welding process the kerning feature is not employed. Simply select a letter, type in the measurements and appearance desired and examine the weld box.

Pick a different letter and control it as desired. Proceed into where it moves the first letter. You can choose how much it overlaps based on your layout. Look carefully at the welding box.

Continue until all letters have been manipulated along with the welding box being evaluated for each.

Preview the phrase. The finished letters will show in the welding box checked as a dark line cut with the lighter lines showing where they are welded. If any connection is a powerful filled letter instead, the welding box was not picked for that particular letter. Simply return and decide on the letter and check the welding box.

Welding is one of the most basic and popular jobs in the Cricut Design Studio. Practice the steps above and you will be on your way to using the Cricut in an entirely new way. If you are more of a visual learner, most step by step guides to welding between screenshots are available online.

Cricut machines help people a great deal with making scrapbooks. If it weren't for this particular instrument, folks would probably be cutting designs that they've assembled manually and that would require some rather careful hands. One mistake and that's likely to change the overall theme of your scrapbook. Furthermore, there are resources that you can use along with a few Cricut machines that may make the whole process a lot easier. One of them is the Cricut Design Studio software and Cricut mats.

Some people today confuse the Cricut method as the one directly accountable for creating the designs. That is a very major problem. The thing responsible for the designs are the software programs and that is the point at which the Cricut layout studio software comes into play.

This software tool includes lots and a lot of designs which are jazzy and could suit anyone's taste. The best thing about the app tool is the fact it grants the user rights to edit the designs it currently has and to create new ones.

It additionally has Internet service which permits Internet upgrades to your software. If you find new designs that are accessible on the Internet, you can add them to an app's library at the push of a button. The Cricut layout studio software is priced at $60. Search the Net with this program and it will provide you a few links where you can download the software from. And then, we have got Cricut mats.

The mat is responsible for holding the paper or vinyl you'll have the Cricut machine trimming your style on. This can be a very sticky piece of paper that is very like a ribbon pad. If you are not experienced in the process for applying this particular mat, then you're likely to end up buying more than you expect.

A fantastic approach to ensure the sturdiness of your mat is to cover it. Nearly all the time, the user fails to cover the mat after this and use lets lots of dust particles sit on the top layer of the mat. If you've got one pad, then use a translucent plastic to protect it. If you are using two, you might continue to keep both face to face. If your Cricut mats have lost their stickiness, you can use a decorative spray on to let it regain its adhesiveness. It's been tried and tested so you do not have to be concerned about doing this.

If you're a scrapbooker with a great deal of good ideas that you just don't necessarily know how to get out on paper, take into consideration the cost of Cricut Design Studio. This super software program can permit you to turn all of your fantastic ideas into magical creations right before your eyes.

You can find numerous top scrapbook designs and themes around.

You can find out about cartridges and also how to use these as well as how to use more than one cartridge on your design. Find out about the outside mat, as well as how to use it so as to generate the best designs for your scrapbook themes.

Organize everything in your own cartridge library and you can always get it if you desire it. You can add keywords to your library to make it a whole lot simpler to find just what you would like and a whole lot more. These are just a few examples of all of the things the Cricut Design Studio may do for you personally.

There is a small learning curve in regard to using the program, nevertheless, and additionally the manual it includes does not do an excellent job of describing things. Luckily there are a couple great, helpful tutorials and guides available on the market written by other people using the program that could aid you with creating a Cricut Design Studio job.

The minimum system requirements include:

OS = Windows 7

Processor rate = 1800 MHz

Ram = 512 MB

Free hard disk space = 100 MB

Topical media drive = CD/DVD-ROM

USB port = 1.1

Display resolution configurations = 1024x768 or higher

It is essential to be sure your computer meets these minimum requirements before investing in this application. When you know you meet the requirements and you get the program on your own, all you want to do is begin using it to make the best designs around for your own scrapbooks.

Cricut is the brand-new a choice of personal digital cutting machines specializing in the very cutting edge of things for home decoration, scrapbooking, paper cutting, card making, and much more. Whatever you might do with a Cricut is simply restricted by your own imagination. These machines include Cricut cartridges for easy use. The cartridges include numerous amazing built-in templates for many different uses and sizes. This gadget is also quite straightforward to maintain. The designs can be chosen from the cartridge or may be custom made using the Cricut Design Studio to take your creativity to great heights - but a computer is required for this particular purpose.

The Cricut bundle comprises these:

Cricut machines: All these are the sources which do the actual cutting based on your creative designs.

Gypsy: This really is really the total Cricut cartridge library in one go. It is a hand-held device that includes the total Cricut layout studio - to ensure anytime you want to run on a design the gypsy is handily offered.

Cricut Design Studio: It is the full-fledged program for producing any design on a Cricut cutter. All you'll need is a computer. Additionally, it may be used to easily investigate, cut and design from the entire cartridge library. The program also lets you save the design for future needs. Assessing a Cricut design has never been easier!

Cuttlebug: It is the personal die cutting and embossing system. It features different sizes and styles like paper-crafting, house decoration, home tasks, events, and faculty jobs. The program is designed by leading artists and offers sharp die cuts every time. Cuttlebug additionally includes professional exceptional embossing for connections with its various textures and sizes, making it a wonderful system.

Cricut Cake: This is an optional tool used for producing designer confectioneries for sandwiches and cakes and other snacks, in almost no time.

Cricut Expression: An advanced version called the Cricut Expression can be used for sheets as big as 24" x 12." Additionally, it includes cartridges and advanced possibilities, like the adding of colours, printing, plus far more, making it ideal for many jobs.

Cricut is the handicraft enthusiast's best buddy, or for anyone who wants to design and create. It supplies over 250 distinct designs in a variety of sizes. The designs can be bigger than an inch or larger than about 11 inches. The different cutting angles offer precision reduction - all of this together with templates that are appealing along with stylized alphabets, provides much to select from.

KNOWING THE MATERIALS TO USE WITH CRICUT

The Cricut personal electronic cutter must be recognizable to anyone at anybody interested in home crafts, and especially scrapbooking. If you're a newcomer to the entire world, then suffice it to say the Cricut personal electronic cutter is a truly revolutionary cutting tool which can effortlessly cut any shape or design it is possible to consider. By the time you've read this guide, you should develop into someone who is much more knowledgeable on what this system (or more precisely, this variety of machines) can provide you.

The intention of the guide is to deliver an easy five-step procedure you can use so as to use a Cricut personal electronic cutter to make a visually stunning design. I will flesh out each of the steps with the thought processes you may encounter, and the choices you are going to need to make. After all, you are going to be able to go off and make something that's currently based on your own creativity.

Have an idea

The first step to creating your masterpiece is an idea. However, complicated by the technology you're using, it is useless if you don't have any inspiration to start with. It might possibly be that you understand exactly what it is you are trying to make - say a scrapbook page on your kid's college sports day or possibly a family reunion. You may not be so certain - in case, I urge a speedy look on Google for "scrapbooking websites" or something similar. Have a browse through a couple of those websites and you are likely to find almost endless inspiration extremely fast.

Which Cricut?

If you do not already have a Cricut personal electronic cutter - then you are going to need to decide at this stage which one fulfils your needs. Your choice will probably be based upon your budget, and if you are going to need anything more than fundamental cutting purposes. The precise information about what each version can do and the way they are purchased is beyond the scope of this guide, yet this info is publicly accessible online.

Select a cartridge

The following step is to choose an appropriate cartridge from the Cricut options. Again, going into detail concerning the Cricut cartridge procedure is out of scope for this specific post - the very best choice is to go and browse through the numerous accessible cartridges online at Amazon or somewhere similar. You're in a position to buy cartridges with designs and shapes for whatever you might think about. All cartridges are compatible with each Cricut personal electronic cutter variant model.

Customize your cut

With an idea, a system alongside a cartridge setup, you're nearly there. The prior decision-making point would be to choose how you want to customize your design together with the further options available with the Cricut personal electronic cutter. This choice involves the dimensions of this app and works like a page, stretch-to-fit and lots of different men and women.

Hit a button

In the end, all of your job is completed - you should load your paper or card and hit the start button.

Should you abide by those five simple measures, you're in a position to go from a spark of inspiration for your professional jaw-dropping layout in super quick time. I expect you have gotten pleasure in the process and will get the outcome which you are looking for!

TIPS TO HELP YOU START

Capturing memories on a virtual camera, an HD camera, and a voice recorder make life more purposeful. Whenever there is a unique moment which you want to grab and maintain a place to return to at any given time, then you can accomplish this easily with the advice of these tools. But pictures are still the favourite medium by nearly all individuals. If you'd like to put together those pictures and compile them onto a distinguishing souvenir, you then can turn into scrapbooking.

Scrapbooking is a system of preserving ideas which has been in existence for quite some time, and it has evolved to be so much better. Years ago, the creation of one scrapbook was a monumentally crazy job. These days, however, with the introduction of apparatus such as the Cricut cutting machine, things are made much . If you are looking to make one, then this bad boy is the instrument for you. There are great Cricut ideas available on the marketplace that you might get the most out of.

Scrapbooks are only a few of the many Cricut ideas available on the marketplace. This instrument, if you know how to maximize it can assist you in generating items which go beyond scrapbooking such as calendars. If you buy a second-hand cartridge, then you are going to discover a lot of layouts uploaded in each and every one. These pre-generated themes may be used for a great deal of things such as picture frames, and greeting cards.

Only your creativity will limit your advancement using a Cricut device. Along with calendars, you're in a position to lay out every month to be a symbol of the weather, the mood, and special events which are connected with this. The Cricut machine will allow you to look for ideas, however, in the event one cartridge doesn't have the designs you want, you could always go and purchase a different one. It is that easy!

Cricut machines are marginally priced with the cost starting at $299. That's pretty hefty for anyone to begin with. Be a wise buyer. You may turn to the Internet to find good deals. Purchasing from eBay can likewise be a terrific move but can take a lot of risks if you're not experienced with eBay. In the event you're very concerned about that, you may always wait for a sale to occur at one of the regional cities and buy out there as that's going to most likely have a guarantee.

Those are simply some of the numerous amazing Cricut ideas that can be found on the market. Calendars alongside a whole lot of other things can be produced from the usage of this great machine. Bear in mind; only your creativity can limit what you can do.

WHY SHOULD YOU GET A PERSONAL CRICUT CUTTER?

Are you into paper crafting? Can you really do a whole lot of scrapbooking? I have been that person for some time now, and I must say, one of the toughest components was cutting my shapes or letters. It takes forever. Lately, I'd been introduced to the Cricut personal cutter, which is an automatic cutting system which does all of this tedious job for you. I have done a bit of

Explore with this specific solution and was eventually convinced I wanted to buy it. In this column, I shall show the top 5 reason I chose to purchase a Cricut personal cutter.

*Love the simplicity of clipping a range of sizes

Compared to other cutting-edge systems, with the Cricut personal cutter, it is possible to use the system to reduce any sizes of letters or shapes involving 1 to 2 5.5 inches. Formerly, to let me cut specific shapes using a standard die-cut platform I had to get different templates for every single letter and every single size of these letters. The superb thing about my choice to buy the Cricut personal cutter is that I did not need these various templates.

*It's light and easy to carry

The Cricut personal cutter is so easy to carry around, in contrast to other big and hefty die-cut machines. Moreover, you may also purchase a carrying bag for this. You can simply take it into a friends' home and have a scrapbooking party jointly. And if you ever have to move your own Cricut personal cutter, then it won't be an issue in any way.

*It's compact and conserves distance space

After you purchase a Cricut personal cutter, you do not have to prepare a lot of space to keep it in. It's fairly compact and doesn't occupy a significant quantity of space. Moreover, you do not have to experience the issue of keeping dividers for templates, such as with old designed die-cut machines. It is not hard to put your Cricut personal cutter on your desk without it taking up a lot of space.

*It works great for almost any sorts of jobs

Whether you're in the mood to do scrapbooking, or perhaps create a birthday celebration for a friend, or perhaps helping your child with a school job, you can pretty much use your Cricut personal cutter for whatever you would like. It has various shapes and attributes you may use. I must admit, when working together with all the Cricut personal cutters, the instant you get those creative juices flowing, then there are no limitations in what it is possible to create.

*It's automatic and great technology.

Instead of needing to manually cut every letter, the Cricut personal cutter does it automatically. All you have to do is put your paper on the mat, follow a few instructions, and press a couple buttons, together with the cutter can do all the challenging job for you. This truly is an excellent feature since it's likely to set up your personal Cricut personal cutter to start cutting something, and you're in a position to do anything else at the same time. This makes scrapbooking a breeze.

As it is possible for you to see from the high top five reasons I made a choice to purchase a Cricut personal cutter this is a very valuable tool that may allow you to cut a few distinct sizes, but additionally produce any job you want, using its high tech interface. So do not hesitate to take a peek at this superb tool and determine the way the Cricut personal cutter will help save you money and effort in your own papercraft projects like it has helped me.

Being a savvy person has never been easier when using the Cricut Expression 2. This handy-dandy item of gear has made it easy and enjoyable to make your own craft tasks personal and unique to your eyes. Since the Cricut Expression 2 is not the very first of its kind (hence the 2) the brand-new slick design together with the full colour LCD touch screen display with stylus shows its growth along with the times. Let's be fair; we do not need things to just work nicely, we additionally want it to look good too.

Scrapbooking could be of a creative outlet when compared with this hobby along with the many attributes the Cricut Expression 2 supplies you with. But do not make the mistake of thinking you're only limited to scrapbooking because it is possible to use this for almost any creative job you're doing or add to individual jobs that you've previously completed. Together with the Cricut can do, the possibilities are boundless!

Unlike the newest purchases, this tool includes two powerful cartridge's functions like the alphabet cartridge combined with another purpose like the frightening cartridge. The alphabet cartridge is precisely what you'll use for letters, numbers and layouts providing life to anything you write. No longer do you have to settle for plain Jane letters and figures considering that when using the Cricut Expression 2 plain is not ever an option.

Let us discuss the key cartridge. "Why?" you may inquire? Well, allow me to tell you this multi-purpose cartridge is where the imaginative pleasure starts! With this particular cartridge, you're likely to have the ability to acquire a great deal of designs, shapes and artwork that could open your mind and get the creative juices flowing so your jobs can develop into the masterpieces you planned them to become.

Characteristics like mat preview to allow you to see until you commit. Furthermore, there are material preferences, so you can get the job to perfection consequently. Furthermore, you will have a cutting place light to aid with the specific reductions you want done. There is definitely somebody at the Cricut development branch that is trying to please the client!

It consistently means more when you or someone you love makes something from scratch for you because they need to set a fantastic deal of energy and idea behind it to really sit down and create it. The Cricut Expression 2 allows everyone to start a brand-new process of production. In case you have not tapped into your inner craftiness, you have the ability to use the Expression 2 to expand your thoughts to what options you will find. Together with the beauty in this is the freedom you have obtained when using the decision to express yourself with no advice of hallmark or some other significant manufacturing.

Envision how refreshing it is to let yourself understand that you have the capability to show that self-in an artistic manner working together with the Cricut Expression 2. Occasionally we get wrapped up in our everyday lives. We do not take the chance to quantify this from the daily regimen and do something which we can genuinely appreciate. So, stop restricting yourself and start having fun.

CHAPTER TWO

TOOLS AND ACCESSORIES

There are not many supplies you need to get started with your Cricut Explore, and they all arrive with the bundle when you purchase even the most fundamental Cricut Explore package-- which means you do not need to purchase anything extra in the beginning! The two included Cricut accessories are a cutting mat and a carbide blade. Everything else is optional, but make it possible for you to do much more with this wonderful machine! Let us check these out!

MUST-HAVE CRICUT EXPLORE ACCESSORIES

Cricut Explore blades

The Cricut Explore includes a super sharp German carbide fine-point blade so you may start cutting straight away. It's placed within the Cricut and can easily be changed when it dulls. I use the fine-point blade for nearly all my trimming, and it always lasts more than that I expect it to. If you're cutting tough substances, you might find you need to change it more frequently. The home with the blade is silver (old machines) or stone (newer machines). There's also a deep cutting blade, which you will need for cutting heavier stuff, such as thin leather and wood. You will want to acquire the distinct home to it and then swap it from the machine. The home for the profound cut blade is shameful. It is also possible to purchase the blades separately as soon as you have the home.

Ultimately, there's a bonded fabric blade, that you will use to cut fabric that's been coated with heat n bond or another stabilizer.

Note that the Cricut Maker includes a knife blade, a rotary blade, a scoring wheel, a perforation blade, an engraving suggestion, a debossing tip, and a wavy tool--and not one of those tools are compatible with all the Cricut Explore. Have a look at my Cricut Maker accessories article to find out more.

Cutting mats

You will also receive a green 12″x12″ standard grip cutting mat in many Cricut Explore boxes. Some of the more recent machines have the light grip cutting mat. Both of the mats may be used for the majority of your crafting needs—card stock vinyl, etc. If you are using more delicate stuff, such as vellum or mild paper, then you may want to stay with all the light grip mat. If you are cutting heavier materials with an inclination to change, try out a purple strong grip cutting mat. I use my heavier cutting mat to cut chipboard and coated fabric. But the majority of the time I stick with all the green standard grip one.

If you are cutting bigger projects, Cricut additionally has 12 x 24 mats. I really like them for bigger vinyl jobs --I recently cut iron-on vinyl for 15 bags on a single sheet of vinyl with this bigger size, and it moved even quicker.

Regardless of what cutting mat you use; I suggest breaking it in a little bit prior to using it for the very first time. Take off the crystal-clear mat protector and adhere the mat into the very front of your top several times. It is going to pick up some of that lint and, believe it or not; this can help dramatically when removing your job from the mat after it has been cut. It is almost impossible to remove a job easily from a brand-spanking new mat.

Cricut toolset

Some time back, I wrote an in-depth post concerning the Cricut tool set. I will not go into much detail about the weeder, scraper, spatula, tweezers, scissors, trimmer, along with other resources except to state that every one of these tools are so helpful, and if you are likely to get any accessories to your device, I would get a tool collection. Be certain that you read that article about the best way best to use all of the tools!
I also adore (such as love) my XL scraper. I basically do not use my little one --as the XL scraper is indeed much quicker and more successful.

Scoring stylus

If you would like to create cards, boxes, or anything else which needs precise folding, I suggest getting yourself a scoring stylus. This tool fits readily to the Cricut's carriage. The Cricut can hold a blade and scoring stylus at precisely the exact same time so you don't need to swap them out--you can score and cut at precisely the exact same moment! Scoring makes it effortless to fold your own projects. If you use jobs from the Cricut picture library, the grading layer is constructed into any document that has to be folded. Find out more about the scoring stylus.

Cricut pens

One of my absolute preferred accessories are Cricut pens. As soon as I received my own Cricut Explore, I did not realize that it could, besides scoring and cutting, also compose! My favourite use for this to tackle letters and cards. This past year I used my Cricut Explore for addressing Christmas cards, and it worked out great!

Where to buy affordable Cricut supplies

Among the questions I get most often is, "where do I purchase Cricut products cheap?"

The ideal thing to do would be to register to get emails from the Cricut store. They have sales going on all of the time. Vinyl could be 25 percent off for a week--stock up!

Obviously, most of us want to save cash, but a good deal of times shop coupons do not work on Cricut things on the Internet or in the local craft shop. However, be certain that you check the clearance department --you may also frequently find discontinued Cricut equipment available on clearance.

Amazon is always a fantastic spot to try for Cricut products in case you've got Amazon prime shipping (receive a free trial here!)) --

it'll get to your home at no cost! Additionally, assess eBay--individuals frequently sell their equipment there.

How to produce a reverse canvas

Now let us do a job that looks a whole lot tougher than it really is--turning a plain, wrapped canvas into a piece of artwork using the opposite canvas technique! I am partnering with my favourite craft shop Joann with this enjoyable tutorial--you can get whatever you want (and more!) in-store or online!

I have made this adorable "eat, drink, and be merry" for the Christmas season, however this tutorial functions for almost any picture you may want! It is infinitely customizable. Here are only a couple of those things you can switch up when creating your personal reverse picture:

- Paint or stain the framework.
- Use a cut file picture with any sort of iron-on vinyl, such as sparkle, holographic, and much more.
- Use a print afterwards and cut the picture on iron-on vinyl.
- Hand-paint a picture on the canvas.
- Stencil a picture on the canvas.
- Use a "hot jumble canvas" technique.
- Use the framework as a shallow shadowbox for sentimental items such as movie tickets, infant wristbands from the hospital, or photographs.

REVERSE CANVAS SUPPLIES

- Wrapped canvas
- Craft knife
- Acrylic ruler (optional)
- Iron-on vinyl (I used black, pink, and green)
- Easy press mini, easy press, or iron
- Pushpins
- Hot glue gun
- Cricut Design Space file

Reverse canvas instructions

Using the craft knife, carefully remove the canvas from the frame, cutting on the outside of the staples. I find an acrylic ruler makes this really easy.

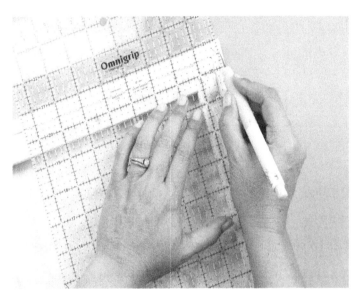

Pull off the canvas and set the frame aside. If you want to paint or stain the frame, now is a good time to do that so it can dry while you do the rest of your project.

Cut your image using your Cricut. I decided on a cute "eat, drink, and be merry" file in Design Space (link in the supply list). Remember to reverse your iron-on vinyl before cutting and place the shiny side of the iron-on vinyl on the mat.

Centre your image on your canvas. It doesn't have to be perfectly centred—you'll have some wiggle room later in the process. Stick it using your preferred heat source. I'm using my easy press mini, which works perfectly for small projects like this.

Then repeat with the remaining two layers.

Center your canvas behind the frame. You'll see here that though I thought my canvas was straight, I ended up off-centering it a bit to get it squared up in the frame. Once centered, carefully flip the frame over.

Without shifting the canvas, pin the canvas to the back. This just helps you keep it lined up as you glue.

Starting in one corner, hot glue the canvas to the inner part of the frame, keeping the canvas taut.

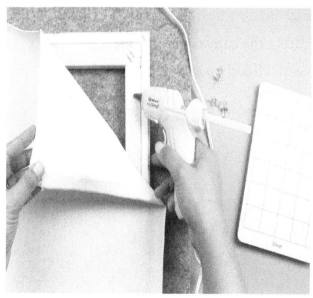

Using the craft knife, trim off the extra canvas. I find the channel between the two parts of the frame makes a perfect guide for cutting off the back. If you want, you can cover the back with felt for a more finished look.

Flip it over and admire your handiwork! I love that this project looks much more complicated than it is. These reverse canvases are perfect for Christmas gifts for friends, family, and even neighbours!

CHAPTER THREE

PRODUCING CRICUT STENCIL USING STENCIL BLANK

When it comes to particular craft classes, I get so many requests for earning home decor hints employing the Cricut. There are many methods to do so --now I am sharing the way to cut a stencil sterile and use paint. In the forthcoming weeks, I will also be discussing how to create a Cricut stencil together:

Cricut stencil vinyl

Cricut adhesive vinyl

Freezer paper

You can also use iron-on vinyl on timber, which will be my taste --no mess!

But let's get cracking with this method--using stencil vinyl to create a stencil along with your Cricut Explore or Cricut Maker. You may find whatever you want to produce this job at the regional Joann or even online! I'm particular to purchasing online this season --I would rather have the wonderful email carrier deliver me my equipment compared to heading out in the rainy weather!

Cricut stencil supplies

Green standard grip or purple strong grip mat

Wood craft framework

Stencil blank

Roll of masking tape

Craft paint in a number of colours such as white

Sponge stipple brushes

Little, rigid paint brush

Paint tray

Merry & bright SVG

Mine arrived painted with a white backing board. If yours doesn't, you can hide the frame and paint the backing board white (or a different color if you want). You may stencil right on the raw timber, but you cannot actually fix jelqing in wood. It is possible, however, to use paint to touch up any bleeds on a painted sign. It is your choice!

CRICUT STENCIL DIRECTIONS

Earning the stencil in Cricut Design Space

Create a new job in Cricut Design Space. On the left, click upload. Subsequently, navigate to this file you downloaded above.

Click Save.

Then choose the document you uploaded and then click on "insert images" to fetch it onto your own canvas.

I might have given you a real stencil record, but I needed to be sure you learned the procedure for turning a normal clip file into a stencil. Be aware you are going to want to use a stencil font, so the inside of your letters remain attached to a stencil.

Begin by clicking shapes from the left design panel and picking a square.

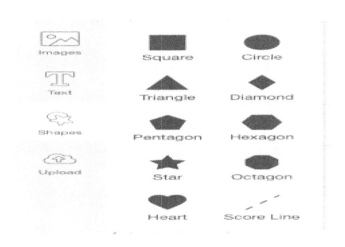

Then alter the dimensions of your square foot to match inside your framework. I love to make it around 1/2″ smaller compared to my framework, so I have space to tape it into the backing board so it will not change. In this instance, I left my square 10″ x 10″ since my board is roughly 10.25″ x 10.25.″

So, you can line your square along with your picture correctly, pick the square foot by clicking on it and then send it using the arrange menu in the upper edit toolbar.

You can now line up your picture and the square foot. If you would like, use the align tools from the edit toolbar to be certain everything is recorded correctly.

Now we are going to slice! Slicing may be confusing to new Cricut users. There are two chief principles: 1) You can just cut two things at a time (in this instance, the picture and the square) and,

2) you will have plenty of leftover bits when you are done because you'll notice.

Click on either the square and the picture, then click slice in the base of the Layers panel to the right.

You will notice your layers panel currently includes three "slice results"--a shameful merry & bright, a grey merry & bright, plus a stencil piece. Delete the first two layers, so you're only left with your stencil piece.

Now you are prepared to cut your stencil! You will surely want to perform a little test cutting along with your blanks. I moved through three stencil blanks (folk art brand) until I got a feeling that really worked. You may test my placing, but certainly, make sure it's working before you cut your entire stencil!

Cutting the stencil

Click make it at the top right of your canvas.

There's nothing additional to do from the prepare screen, so click continue.

In case you've got a Cricut, place your dial to habit.

From the make screen, for the Explore or the Maker, click browse all materials and hunt for stencil.

In the bottom, you will see a green connection for material settings. This permits one to fine-tune all your settings. Scroll down to stencil film and switch it into the following settings: 350 strain and 3x multi-cut.

Click Save. You'll need to go back to browse all materials and select stencil film as the material.

Set your stencil picture onto your own mat. Put your mat beneath the guides and press the blinking arrow to fit your mat in your machine.

Press the blinkings along with your Cricut to cut your stencil film. Important: once you turn the mat from your system following the cut, try to be certain it's cut all of the way through. Otherwise, press on the "c" one longer, and it'll cut again. You cannot do so if you choose the mat from this machine, however, so be certain that you inspect the cut together with the mat still in the Cricut.

STENCILLING A HOUSE DECOR SIGN

We can stencil our sign! Begin by taping your stencil into the interior of your framework. You do not need it changing around!

There are a few options here; however, I haven't found either of them work for me personally.

You can dab on a coating of white paint on your stencil. The concept is that the white paint will bleed providing you a crisper line. That is true, except I've discovered that using two coats of paint (the white and the color) can occasionally make my stencil peel once I pull this up. Not necessarily, but it is a risk.

The next is dabbing a layer of mod podge in your stencil. Same concept, but I frequently observe the exact same result, together with my paint really pulling as I lift the stencil. It is possible to play around and see whether one of these choices work for you!

For me personally, I love to go right to the paint. Using sponge daubers, get a small quantity of paint onto the sponge, then dab it on a scratch paper, then paint the stencil. You want to use hardly any paint and use a dabbing motion rather than brushing. This can assist in preventing bleeding.

Continue with this technique for the remaining part of the sign with all the other colors.

Before the paint is actually set, peel back the tape and then carefully lift the stencil (this can keep your paint from sticking and pulling upward).

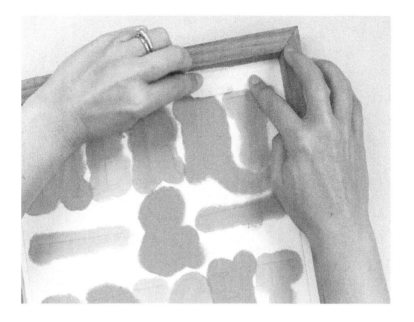

There is a good chance you are still going to have a little bit of bleeding. You can see a little in mine at the underside "r" below.

If you use a small quantity of paint and use a dabbing motion, it ought to be kept to a minimal. Use white paint along with a tiny stiff paintbrush to touch up any areas that require it.

Once dry, it is possible to seal the art with a little poly coating if you would like --but when it is for indoor use, I usually skip this step.

You may use this method to generate all kinds of stencilled signs! This merry & bright sign could be so adorable in a conventional palette of greens and reds, or in place of white chalk on a chalkboard!

CHAPTER FOUR

HOW TO MAKE PERSONALISED PLATES AND MUGS

Create your own mug with vinyl

10 minutes (time spent performing things)

5 minutes (time spent around)

15 minutes (total project time)

Tools

Cricut Explore air and fundamental tools

Scissors

Materials

Exterior glue vinyl in whatever colors you would like (I used silver, slate grey, and dark blue)

Transport tape

"Baby it's cold outside" layout (you can find my Cricut layout here)

Rubbing alcohol

Cotton balls

This Valentine's Day cocktail job is ideal for a "first time" plastic undertaking. Therefore, if you got a Cricut device for Christmas, now's the time to get it from the box and begin creating!

Here is what you will have to create these cute mugs.

- Cricut system (I used my Cricut Explore Air Two; however, you could use any Explore device or the Maker. -- do not stress silhouette users, I still have not forgotten about you! You might even use the SVG document)
- Heat transport plastic -- yes, I will place HTV onto a ceramic mug! What??? Stick around -- you will see!
- Better collectively SVG document (you can find this here)
- Mini handheld iron or heat media using a mug attachment

Here are the ways for the best way to decorate mugs with iron-on vinyl along with a Cricut.

DIRECTIONS

Begin with opening Cricut Design space on your browser and begin a fresh project. Click on the "insert text" button on the left and right type your text to the new text box. On the right, below the "edit" tab, you can change the font and size and orientation of your text if you want. I changed the font to wildflower.

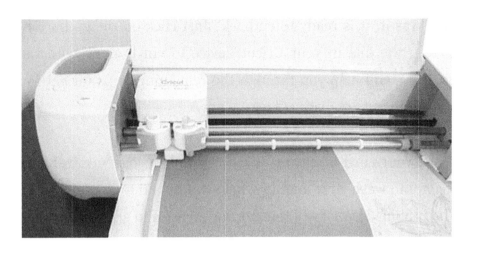

I then clicked "insert images" and discovered a cute snowflake I enjoyed and added it. I resized the picture so it would match on the mug and put it under my text.

That was it; it is ready to cutback! Just click on the go button, placing the dial in your Cricut device to vinyl, along with the program, will help you through the remaining steps for cutting and loading every distinct layer of vinyl.

While your vinyl is cutting, use a cotton ball soaked in rubbing alcohol to wash your mug in which you intend to set your vinyl. The rubbing alcohol will remove any grease and grime from your fingers so the plastic sticks.

Once your vinyl is cut, weed off any desktop vinyl using the weeding tool, leaving the letters and layout on the backing paper.

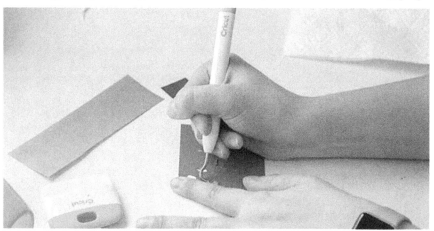

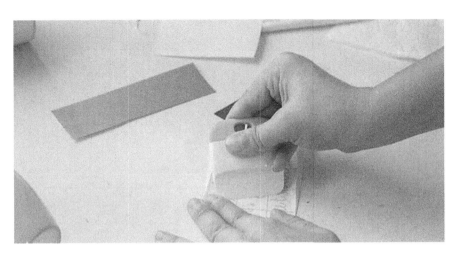

Then trim a slice of tape to exactly the identical dimensions as your vinyl layout. Remove the backing paper in the transport tape and stick the tape onto your vinyl layout. Use the scraper tool to actually press the tape onto the vinyl, so it sticks.

Gently peel the tape; it must follow the vinyl nicely enough to lift up the letters off the backing paper. Then place the vinyl layout on your mug, using the scraper tool to actually stick the vinyl letters onto the mug.

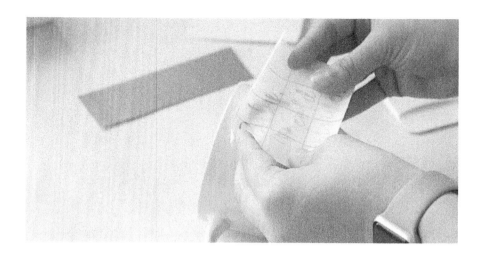

When the vinyl is actually stuck onto the mug, then gently peel back the tape, leaving the vinyl letters onto the mug. And you are done!

Fill it with your favourite hot drink and revel in it!

I propose hand-washing your mug; the dishwasher can be really tough on your dishes and also the vinyl letters might begin to peel off after repeated washing.

CHAPTER FIVE

MORE CRICUT MACHINE ACTIVITIES

Crafting hobbyists

Crafting is just among those most famous hobbies in the world today. You can find a lot of men, women and even kids who like crafting and a few who make a professional living from it. You'll discover a great deal of special tools, software and supplies programs accessible to assist these crafting fans make the most of the moment.

The Cricut system is just that. It's a digital cutter which aids with papercrafts. With only a small button, you'll be able to create lovely designs and receive help with crafts like home decor, artwork, paper crafting and much more. This system is quite simple to navigate and use so that the one thing you really must be concerned about is being imaginative and empowering your imagination to run rampant.

There's no need to get a PC to use the Cricut device. All you will need is a typical electrical outlet to plug it into, and you're prepared to proceed. Before you begin, it's beneficial to take a little time and get more comfortable with this particular machine. Have a peek in the paper feed to comprehend how everything functions.

The on button, clip button and stop button will be grouped together on the right of this device, the newspaper feed is in the back.

To begin, first find the crafts you want to work on. Put a Cricut cartridge into the device, and you also get to select from several layouts, measurements and find each detail of the fashion. You will find countless hundreds of ideas, so the layouts you're ready to create with your crafting are going to be unlimited.

There's a user manual that includes the machine you can look through if you're experiencing any issues. The Cricut method is actually a priceless investment for any crafter who chooses takes their particular hobby seriously.

Using Cricut cutting machines on craft projects

A growing number of people are choosing to create their very own scrapbooking materials, cards and invitations. These do-it-yourself choices allow a fantastic deal and give you more room for customization compared to their own mass-produced options. Not only are homemade invitations a good deal more customizable, but they also cost less than shop-bought options. Cricut private cutting machines also make it possible for those who have minimal time and much less expertise to create professional-looking craft jobs anytime.

Cricut cutting machines are available anyplace in craft shops alongside department stores which contain artwork and art segments. On the other hand, the absolute best bargains are usually found on the Internet. For your occasional do-it-yourself, the entrance level variant, together with easily available sale costs of approximately $100 is more than adequate. It's more than capable of developing a huge variety of distinct shape mixes and needs hardly any maintenance. More seasoned crafters, or people who handle home companies that create customized paper goods, may discover that bigger models are somewhat more depending on their own requirements.

These machines are automatic, and also a good deal easier to use than manual paper cutters. Normally, they can cut quite heavy paper stock, allowing scrapbookers to create layouts that have several different colors and textures. For advice about the best approach to use a system, you will find a choice of websites offering information from frequent amateur customers.

They're a substantial source for inspiration and information, demonstrating the way the system may be best employed. Those websites are a terrific destination for the ones just beginning, the best feature of a house Cricut machine is it has the capacity to make completely one-of-a-kind pages. Experiment with new forms and color combinations to make something distinctive and memorable.

Cricut cutting machines are adaptable and can be used for just about any type of craft project.

Make professional hunting scrapbooks using Cricut personal cutting machines

A Cricut cutting machine can be a vital requirement for any scrapbooker. These machines also make it possible for clients to cut paper to a variety of intriguing shapes, making personalizing each page in a scrapbook simple and pleasurable. Made to be small enough to go with you when you travel, they'll occupy little space in your house and may be carried out with you for virtually any scrapbooking celebrations you may attend. They're the ideal tool for everybody who's searching for a user-friendly way of producing specific borders, sew or other page designs.

Cricut machines can make shapes which are anywhere from 1" to over 5" tall. Simple to alter metal cutting patterns are used to make uniform shapes on several kinds of artwork paper. These include custom decoration, joyous shapes or intriguing borders that could reflect the content of every page. As many identifying thicknesses of card stock may be used, scrapbookers must take note that paper in a lower grade might cause the blades to dull faster. This typically implies you want to always keep a tab on the sharpness of the blade and then replace them if needed to maintain results which are exceptional.

A Cricut machine isn't a small investment. Prices start at roughly $100 online, which might put this cutting-edge device from reach to get a couple of. However, once taking under consideration the price of buying packs of pre-cut shapes and letters, most dedicated scrapbook fans do find the apparatus will eventually pay for itself. It could also be used for additional paper crafts, like making custom invitations, gift tags and cards. The Cricut firm has a fantastic standing in the business world, and their goods are certainly likely to last a long time; therefore, no replacement ought to be required, despite heavy usage.

Scrapbooking is getting more popular than ever with the use of Cricut cartridges. Creating a scrapbook might be enjoyable for the whole family. It's an innovative means to keep family history with photos, journal entries, in addition to memorabilia. Implementing a Cricut expression cutting machine with its massive library of Cricut cartridges makes past images come home to a future generation!

Soon agreeing to the production of photos, people began producing ideas of this way kind to keep the photographs. From the 15th century as when cheap newspaper became accessible to the average citizen in England, scrapbooks known as scrapbooks were kept to put quotations, poetry, correspondence, together with recipes.

Afterwards as now, each scrapbook was unique to the writer's specific theme. From the 16th century, friendship documents were the rage. These records were like modern-day yearbooks, where buddies sign each other's yearbook at the end of the college year.

All those virulent outlets afforded girls in succeeding generations with chances to develop their literacy skills by reproducing their own personal history. It may be difficult for people to imagine now, but women living prior to the 18th and 19th centuries normally didn't possess the ability to read and write made easily available for them.

The producers of Provo craft certainly don't want to have these days return when girls were kept in the dark! In reality, they churn out inventions annually with each passing year to bring our creativity to light. As an example, the handy Cricut Jukebox was created for scrapbookers to conveniently preserve nearly all those Cricut cartridges effortlessly. Implementing the jukeboxes, there's not any need to prevent your creative stream if you would really like to change cartridges out.

Besides the recently published Old West and Hannah Montana, you'll find wonderful classics like a Disney Mickey font cartridge alongside Christmas Solutions cartridge. Two of my favourites, which I've been astounded at the activities results, would be the Home Accents solutions cartridge along with also the Home Decor solutions cartridge. In case you've ever wondered exactly what Provo craft indicates by boundless chances within their motto have a look at these impressive cartridges!

Use your Cricut machine to make money scrapbooking

If you are into scrapbooking at all then no doubt you've learned about Provocraft's Cricut cutting machines. They're amazing machines which take an excellent deal of effort out of plenty of jobs, do not take a computer to use, and they're so straightforward and intuitive to understand how to use! In the event you've ever used one, then you probably have noticed precisely just how much fun they are, but have you thought about how to earn money doing what you really love?

Earning money out of this passion is really a fantasy of all; however, they generally think that it is too hard and give up. The easy truth is that doing so is not really that hard! The only limitation is the creativity and what it is likely to create. Here's a few suggestions to get you started with the process to make additional money with your hobby:

Decorate themed parties

Children like to have themed celebrations. When it's a Pokémon celebration, a Bakugan birthday celebration or a Disney character costume party, children just love them. You may easily make some money by creating decoration packs for these sorts of events. Print and cut out a great deal of different sized decorations, and create customized title tags which the children can adhere, produce playing cards in addition to character cards that the youngsters can collect and swap together.

Custom made cards and invitations

Who does not love a personalized thank you card or invitation? It reveals a whole lot of love and thought has gone into them. If you love doing so, why don't you market some of those creations to earn a little cash at precisely the same moment? It's actually surprising how a great deal of individuals want to acquire a custom-made card or invitations created for birthdays, anniversaries, birthdays, anniversaries, get-togethers, and other occasions. Fairly often your local arts and crafts shop are prone to place your creations for sale and show them to their clientele. Apparently, they frequently take a cut, but additionally it saves you the time of needing to go out and find people yourself.

Custom made scrapbook layouts

Scrapbooking can lead to an obsession collectively. We are always trying to create this fantastic page design, or find that perfect touch which may make our scrapbooks that much better. You can use this Cricut method to create die cuts of listing page designs and market them to other fans all on your own. If it is your passion, then it won't be any trouble thinking up a few to-die-for layouts!

Create a site
You may consistently promote your goods online. Nowadays it's fairly straightforward to make an online website. Go to blogger.com and register to get a completely free site, then with just a little practice you'll be able to yield a superb little site featuring each of the fantastic products which you supply. Put it onto a business card (also free using tons of these online offers from the market) and send it out to anyone that you match. They easily have the ability to how off everything you provide in one location and make a buy.

All these are only a few ideas you can use to get started making cash with your hobbies. Do not be intimidated and believe you're not good enough or it's too hard. Just begin trying, and you might end up amazed at exactly how great your attempts turn out.

Cricut scrapbook number one idea

The number one greatest idea to use your Cricut on would be to make something for your little ones!

Children like to follow all types of tales. Yet one story they likely would love to listen to over and over again could be the story of their birth. That is why, many may prefer creating baby scrapbook to show in a more concrete fashion how they were born. However, it doesn't imply that baby scrapbooks are restricted to the "how" of giving birth. Some small details are critical to generate a far more striking baby scrapbook your kid will like and be extremely proud of as they grow. And because a baby scrapbook is a very small child's bibliography, your children are going to love precisely how much they mean to you personally.

Having a newborn infant in the household is pleasurable. Each day the infant will look marginally different from the preceding day as it grows so quickly. One way to keep these intriguing memories alive is to make a baby scrapbook. Along with the scrapbook you're likely to have the ability to examine it in case you need to and can share it with your family and friends.

If you're planning to use your Cricut device to create a scrapbook for the baby ahead, then here are a couple of things that you've got to consider so you won't confine yourself by developing a baby scrapbook which merely tells the time of birth, measurements and weight of your infant.

To make a baby scrapbook, you need to specify your beginning point. It could be the baby shower or possibly the day of the baby's birth. Moreover, you need to set when to finish the scrapbook. Normally, a baby scrapbook will show the child's first year however, you could go longer in the event you'd really like to. In the process, you want to accumulate things that may be contained in the scrapbook such as the presents you get at your baby shower. Some can even include the infant's first haircut along with various events which the child did for the very first time.

Elect to use a color that may establish the topic of this scrapbook. The standard colour of a baby boy's album is powder blue, while the infant girl's album is pink. You may or might not use these colors and could use another.

You request: "What picture should I include from the listing?"

Many baby scrapbooks could include the facts about the infant upon arrival. All these are the time of birth, weight, time of arrival, the length of labor, the colour of their hair and eyes, and physician's name and the titles of the group who helped the physician at the birth. And naturally, the images of you and your kid in the hospital once you gave birth.

Some contain images of you because you're pregnant. Moments like this can help keep your kid learn how you personally, as a mom cared for him before he was born.

Additional things you want to include are the photographs of the infant's development month by month using a dimension reference (normally a stuffed toy), photographs of the home you reside in and also the nursery, photographs of their family members enjoying the infant, photographs of the infant sleeping, photographs taken while the infant is bathing, photographs with their favourite toys, and extra joyous moments that include them.

As was mentioned earlier, many baby scrapbooks could incorporate the baby's firsts. All these would be your baby's first smile, first bathroom crawl, first roll over, first sat up, first steps, etc. Baby scrapbooks may include their favourites such as their favourite tune, toys, bedtime stories, etc.

The nice thing about this is that you may always add whatever is connected to your child as he or she's growing up.

Added vital events which may or might not be captured by memorabilia may be written in the book.

You may write about the significance and value of this title, your length of stay in the hospital, additional men and women who were current in the hospital, their particular response when you gave birth, and their own feelings the minute they delivered your baby, and also the way in which they amuse the infant. Perhaps you will write about stories that may further exemplify these occasions which are recorded in photos. Stories such as the infant's very first moments, babysitting, together with mannerisms (did he or she suck their thumb... And things such as individuals in their life).

You have obtained the photographs, what items to write about and also the scrapbook to put it together; what is next?

Well, creating baby scrapbook is genuinely a personal thing. It is your decision what other items that you would like to integrate so your kid will know precisely how he or she developed.

Some of the benefits of owning the Cricut machine is the fact that it was created for in home use. It's somewhat expensive but worth the cost. My partner was fortunate enough to find it available for $179.99. Provocraft provides a storage bag that's on wheels so you may take it to scrapbook cropping courses or scrapbook celebrations. Its cartridge based and contains a huge variety of styles of letters, phrases and shapes to choose from. The Cricut cartridges marketplace costs approximately $90.00. The cartridges feature an overlay that's set onto the Cricut apparatus. These overlays provide you a number of 3-D effects. A number of them are proof, tags, charms, shadowing, positive and negative imaging. Everything is done right from the touch of a button. It is only restricted to one's creativity.

You can cut the picture as little as 1" or as big as 5 ½." It is likely to use many different thicknesses of paper, but I have a propensity to use more of a moderate card stock. The cutting knife is much more elastic. There's an anxiety setting for thicker papers. Additionally, a rate setting for how quickly you'd like it to cut back. There's an expansion port for future updates. The replacement components for the body are rather pricey. As an instance the cutting mats can be purchased 2 in a bundle for $10.00.

The die cutting machine will not feature everything you want to start. I would have to play with it a little because there is a learning curve. By way of example, for thinner paper you should use the lower rate or it will tear the paper. Another instance, for thicker paper you are most likely to have to fix the blade and place the rate button on a cut. Whenever you're accustomed to it, then it gives you plenty of enjoyment to use it. I especially adore the fact you're all set to rate the expired discounts for simple paper piecing methods. The ideas you are in a position to get for fresh scrapbook page designs are infinite.

Some of the drawbacks are you can't personalize your own die cuts. You may just use what's on the cartridges. The mat that communicates with the die cutting equipment is sticky. I discovered the stickiness wears off immediately. For the mat I use a repositionable spray adhesive. You're restricted to using only real card stock paper. Whatever brand you choose. The blade can't cut any additional substances. I truly like to create chipboard monograms and I'm unable to this using this method.

No wonder they predict it gives Christmas cheer. This cartridge has many intriguing shapes which allow you to truly feel airy and joyful. If you aren't in the Christmas spirit yet, this cartridge certainly offers you the jump start you need. From a grinning reindeer to bits of candy, you will have the ability to decorate your scrapbook pages and you also can't overlook Santa and his sleigh.

All the Cricut cartridges have work keys nevertheless, the one I enjoy the most with this particular cartridge is your position card feature. Every one of the shapes which are on the cartridge are easily accessible to place on a place card, making it ideal for an adult dinner party to your kid's play bash. Whatever celebration you are having, you can make place cards for your guests that will ensure they feel unique.

There's also a label feature. It is not crucial to go and buy gift tags this season for your presents. Just take out this cartridge, your favourite paper, some ribbon and create your own. Now that is going to be a saver for a single pocket simply by producing them yourself. If you are like me you would not even have to buy the equipment, then they are based alongside your "crafting stash of bits."

I just thought of a very adorable idea. If you're creating a scrapbook and possess a border of Christmas lights which are united with slender decoration. (I'd need to do this properly now) it's possible to have a glance at my website in order to see how adorable it was and it just took me around 10 minutes from start to finish.

Additionally, I made Santa a location card to depart with his cookies on Christmas Eve. You may find dozens and dozens of items you will have the ability to produce with this Cricut cartridge. You merely need some imagination and some Christmas cheer to get you crafting.

Scrapbooking is straightforward and just about anybody can get it done. There are essentially 3 jobs and if you do them well you will have the ability to generate a superb scrapbook. These three jobs include organizing photographs, devising designs, and prep workspace. Here are some steps to generate your own scrapbook.

First you need to determine the subject you may use. You'll come across a great deal of potential topics it's possible to pick from. A fast-online study gets your creative juice flowing. What I typically like to do would be go to images.google.com and hunt for scrapbooking topics to find out what other individuals do. And do not neglect to get ideas from other household members. By considering all the ideas from several people you will run into a few wise insights regarding the best approach to make the entire scrapbook look great.

One thing you may find hard in case you haven't done any scrapbooking would be to find pictures. If you're into scrapbooking and are likely to make a great deal of scrapbooks, then you might elect to invest in a digital cutter such as the Cricut personal cutting machine. With help from a computer you will be able to produce all types of shapes and contours. But to start with you can simply use oblong or circle sized templates and subsequently cut the pictures by hand so they are prepared for the scrapbook. It is easy to find these templates in the regional craft shops. Be certain you do a few practice cuts on scrap papers before doing it on the real image. This may be one thing which you don't wish to hurry, as a wrong cut will harm the image and it might be permanent. Also be sure you use a sharp blade so you get a clean edge with a single fold.

Scrapbooking is no doubt among the most interesting things you can do. It will bring back all of the intriguing memories the moment you look at it decades later. These memories are priceless and can't be traded for anything else. A well-done scrapbook may be rewarding enough to be passed down for centuries.

The best way to remove vinyl decals

Decals have become a fairly common attachment for houses, vehicles, and a great deal more. With machines such as Silhouette and Cricut which can be found on the current market, it's simple for everybody to create and design their very own stickers. While we are busy sticking and putting our stickers onto things, many don't think about what they will do after the decal has worn out and they no longer desire it. So, while some are providing the best way how to produce and install stickers, we believed it may be an excellent concept to explain out how to eliminate them this time around.

Heat:

Much like most sticky stuff, heating up the outside can let you remove the decal considerably simpler. When working on a car, you may set it in the sunlight to get a bit hot, and that should be sufficient to get the process moving. Many installers choose to use hairdryers or heating guns, and these certainly are a simpler option if working inside. Just make certain not to make the things too hot with the heating since you do not need to get the scraping. Constantly work in segments, as heating up the whole surface at once will probably be a significant waste of time because the minute you enter another segment, it's very likely to get chilled.

Scrape:

When you have implemented the warmth, you have to be to start scraping the plastic. With this specific component I use a plastic razor blade or credit card. Do not use metal! This is merely very likely to cause harm to anything your decal is on (especially vehicles). You do not have to scratch the whole decal back, only enough to have the ability to get a good grip onto it and peel it off.

Peel:

When you have the boundaries peeled up, you have the capacity to start peeling off the material. You should really get this done slowly, as fast motions will probably make the substance tear or leave extra glue behind. I also advise you to get this done at about a 120-degree angle to start ripping and this can ensure you remove the entire decal simultaneously.

Remove the goo:

Once you are finished removing the decal, you're probably going to see a dirty/sticky outline of where your decal was. You will find an assortment of special products you might use to eliminate this, but I'm a lover of Goo Be Gone. Make sure you read the back of the bottle prior to use to be certain it won't result in certain discolouration or damage to some stage you're working on till you begin. I use the liquid with a terry cloth since it's harder and will work better to remove any grime. You might choose to wipe down the surface a few times, but in the very long run you want to get a new and pleasant surface ready for an upcoming decal project!

CHAPTER SIX

EDITING CRICUT PROJECTS

Cricut Design Space doesn't autosave your endeavours, therefore (as a wonderful practice), I advise you to save your project after you place the exact first piece, shape, or image on the canvas area. Sometimes, tasks can take some time, and if you do not save your job while you can, your valuable time and precious work will pay a visit to the trash if Design Space crashes.

I've lost a few minutes before studying my lesson, so, please save as you go. Notice: "I save modifications in my job every five minutes or so.

When you start on a brand-new canvas, then the save option (found in the upper right-hand corner of the window) will probably be greyed out, however whenever you put in a picture, it's likely to activate.

To save your project, put the very first thing (text, picture, contours, etc.) You can use it on your own canvas.

When you click save, a little window will pop up asking you to name your job. If you are just using Cricut pictures or fonts, then you are going to have the option to discuss your work on Facebook or perhaps Pinterest.

But if you use your own pictures, subsequently the "public" option will not appear. Don't worry though; you are still able to see your creations in the "my tasks" window which will I show you later on.

After naming your project, click on save. A blue banner advertisement will appear with this window, notifying you that the job is saved.

Now, you can start altering your design by integrating text, or changing colors. In this circumstance, I just altered the color of the file. Nothing complicated.

Just remember to store your work every three to five minutes; believe me, you don't want to waste time in the event the app crashes.

If at any period you would like to produce a new job, make sure your job is saved. No worries, however.

If for any reason you still have unsaved modifications, Design Space may deliver a warning.

Don't take this warning lightly; in the event you click on "replace" instead of "save" you will lose your hard work. It happened to me personally, and it might happen to you!

Openwork at Cricut Design Space desktop

To start a project, you've established, you want a clean and fresh new canvas.

Currently, there's not a method for you to mix jobs. Let's hope Cricut adds this functionality soon.

It is likely to discover your designs in two different manners. The first and fastest one is by simply clicking on the "my projects" shortcut found in the right corner of the window.

The next method is by clicking the projects option on the left of the image and see the drop-down menu and then choose the option "my projects" (read the several options of the drop-down menu to find prepared cut jobs).

As you can see on the screenshot above, the job I created is right there. The arrangement of those jobs is predicated on the previous date.

From the "my projects" view, you can edit, delete, customize, and reduce your previously established tasks.

There are different areas when you can click on a particular job; if you click on the "share" choice, you will be motivated to devote a description, photos, etc. And if you click on the 3 dots (bottom-right of each task), then you are going to be able to delete it manually.

If you want to personalize your job or delete it at once, then you'll have to click on the featured image of your design.

Upon clicking a tiny window will open, and you'll have the ability to talk about and see all of the information concerning the task, like the fonts, shapes, and images you have used.

First and foremost, from this window, you have the ability to personalize your work or send it to cut. The "make it" shortcut is great as though your project has been created, it's possible to bypass all the Design Space process and see the mat preview right away.

However, in the event that you want to edit the appearance of your design, click personalize.

Now let's find out how to edit your own undertaking!

Edit projects in the Cricut Design Space desktop

Once you click customize for any job, you have the ability to edit and change things around.
Take a peek at the following screenshot to see the alterations I made to the original design.

Insert form: Add a circle to the image and change color.

Weld: Select the first image and click on the weld tool (bottom of the layers panel) to acquire all our design in 1 layer.

Twist: Place the plotted image in the middle of the ring then pick either ring and then click on the slice tool (together with the weld tool).

Keep the purple ring with a cut-out picture.

This editing is simple. I'm confident you can do it, but just what I wanted to show is the best way to proceed after editing work.

Here's the product, if you click rescue you will revaluate your primary design and if this is what you need, great. However, if you still want to keep the job you started with, click on save and select the choice "save."

Once you click "save" you're going to be motivated to modify the name of your primary project; in this scenario, I just added a "2" to the title.

Easy, right?

But should you decide to use either design again, return to your own jobs and you'll see some are easily available.

Save, open & edit projects out of the Cricut Design Space app (iPad, phone).

The steps you need to store, edit it, and then begin work in Cricut's app are incredibly similar to those that you would make from the PC.

You can find it out fairly quickly, but I want to inform you I grew several white hairs searching for each among the options, so here I am to make it easy for you.

Let us find out together!

Save project in the Cricut Design Space program

The Cricut Design Space app contains three particular viewpoints: home, canvas, and produce.

Ordinarily, when you start the app, the option is going to be placed on "home." To start focusing on a brand-new job, click on the blue square with and sign then tap "canvas."

To be able to save your job, you need to place at least 1 item (kind, text, image). For purposes of this tutorial, I used the image #m44919.

After placing a product, then tap the save icon found on the upper-left corner of this plan and select the choice "save."

When you tap save a little window will pop up in which you'll be able to enter the name of your work, and where you'd love to conserve your own endeavour.

Choose "save to the Cloud" if you want to enter your jobs from the computer, and you have got a reliable online connection. Choose "save iPad/iPhone" in the event that you don't have reliable Internet and appreciate having the capacity to work offline.

When choosing "save iPad," then you won't have the capability to find individual's jobs on your PC. However, you are likely to be able to use that job again and again without access to the Web.

I select "save to the Cloud" because I love having accessibility to my tasks on my personal PC. But by all means, pick whichever matches your needs the best.

Save changes as you operate on your style sense in the event the app crashes, or you might lose all of your hard work.

One thing to consider is the way to start a new job when you have something on your canvas. (it took me a while to figure it out).

Visit the "home" view and tap "new project." If you have unsaved modifications, the application provides a warning. Select previews and save each one of the alterations and repeat precisely the same method to remove any hints.

Don't take this warning lightly; in the event that you don't save, your job will probably be missing.

Openwork in Cricut Design Space program

To begin an already established project, first, make certain your canvas is sterile (no extra jobs, text, design, or shapes) and move into the "house" standpoint of this plan.

With this view, and below your profile picture, there's a drop-down menu, then click and select where your project is (Cloud or iPad/iPhone).

Notice: by that drop-down (additionally if you are connected to the Internet) menu, then you may even find prepared to cut jobs, no current tasks in your system, etc.

As most of my tasks are on the Cloud, so I chose "my jobs on the Cloud."

As you can see in the screenshot down below, I'll find the tasks I have been working on throughout this tutorial.

Outstanding!

From that standpoint, "home/my jobs in the Cloud," you can carry out a couple of things on each undertaking.

Should you tap the "chat" alternative, you will be motivated to create a description, photos, etc. Your own endeavour. And, in the event you click on the 3 dots (bottom-right of each job), then you are going to be able to delete it manually.

If you'd love to personalize your job or delete it at once, then you'll have to tap on the featured image of your design.

Upon tapping the view your phone will change, and you'll be in a position to see all of the information concerning the job, like the fonts, shapes, and images you have got.

First and foremost, from this window, you can personalize your work or send it to cut. The "make it" shortcut is great because when your project has been created, it's possible to bypass all the Design Space process and see the mat preview right away.

However, in the event that you'd love to edit the appearance of your design, click personalize.

Now let's find out how to edit your undertaking!

Edit projects in Cricut Design Space program

If you tap customize for almost any job, you will be able to edit and change things around.

Take a peek at the following screenshot to observe the alterations I made in the original design.

Select all of the letters inside this "daydream outline."

Weld each of the inner letters.

Twist the outline of the coating together with the letters that are welded.

Notice: Slice and weld are inside the action menu.

This editing is very simple, I'm sure you could do considerably better, but precisely what I wanted to show is the best way to proceed after seeing an already recognized undertaking.

In case you tap rescue, then you will revaluate your primary design and if this is what you require great. However, if you still want to keep up the job you started with, click on save and select the choice "save."

Once you click "save" you're going to be motivated to modify the name of your primary project; in this scenario, I just added a "2" to the title.

Easy, right?

Best strategies for picking the ideal Cricut personal electronic cutter

The assortment of Cricut personal digital cutter machines was created to automate lots of those tricky crafting jobs. If you have not heard of these earlier, then keep reading in the event you would like to know how to take your house crafts to the next level. If you're conscious of these, you might be asking yourself how to select which of these cutting machines is suitable for you. Within another guide, I'll be helping you select which one of the four Cricut versions is the best fit for your needs. In the process, you are very likely to comprehend the benefits and pitfalls of each machine, which usually means you are in a position to make an educated choice.

The four models we are most likely to be considering are th standard Cricut personal electronic cutter, the Cricut Create, the Cricut Expression and the Cricut Cake.

The easiest version to try in the start is the Cricut Cake. This was created with a single goal in mind- to create professional-looking decorations. It can cut shapes from bread, fondant, gum paste and other raw materials. It's very much like the Cricut Expression system, but the working parts are changed to make them appropriate for foods. That means parts which have to be cleaned can be readily eliminated. If you are looking to create edible decorations, then that is the only option from the scope. This variant retails from approximately $270.

The other three Cricut personal electronic cutter versions are acceptable for printing. They cut from the exact same substances, such as paper, card, vinyl and vellum. Which version you choose will depend upon your budget and requirements.

Budget

The standard Cricut personal digital cutter is the cheapest priced in the range, costing roughly $100.

Next up is your Cricut Create, starting from $160 and upwards.

The very best of the range of versions is your Cricut Expression, that will set you back about $225.

Prerequisites

All models are compatible with the whole selection of Cricut cartridges. This typically means you've got an almost infinite supply of die cutting layouts, as you can always purchase more cartridges. Therefore, there are two major aspects on your needs to make your pick. These can be the measurements of machine and cuts, in addition to the assortment of die cutting options.

The standard personal electronics cutter and Create machines are small and portable. They will cut contours about 11.5 inches. The Create has a considerably wider variety of capacities.

The Expression is a larger machine, made to get a permanent place in a desk or workbench. It is going to cut up shapes to approximately 23.5 inches, and also employs a huge variety of functions.

By taking into account these factors, you'll have to have the ability to choose the Cricut personal electronic cutter that's best for you.

Individuals really think the Cricut system is one tool that's responsible for the conceptualization of those designs that we find in scrapbooks. In fact, the layouts come from the brain of the consumer and then are made concrete with the Cricut cutting system.

Additionally, there are other tools that make the layouts such as cartridges and software programs. The best software program out there is the Cricut Design Studio. With this system, you can edit and produce your personal designs and edit existing designs which are pre -packaged.

Life is great really! People also feel the use of a Cricut cutting process is only restricted to the topic of scrapbooking. Only a couple people understand that the Cricut machine along with the cartridges and the software tools may possibly be used to make a substantial variety of things. You'll come across a good deal of Cricut projects it is likely to use the Cricut cutting platform for many things and only your mind can restrict what you can do.

Greeting cards are outstanding Cricut jobs for anyone to take part in. With all the layouts you'll have the ability to get in the Cricut cartridge along with the software applications that you've set up, and your layout covers that defy the unconventional. The difficulty that lots of individuals experience when they try to purchase greeting cards is that they cannot track down the kind of the card they're searching for. This may result in anxiety and a fantastic deal of frustration regarding the purchaser's part. You're a whole lot better off creating your own greeting cards.

Cricut calendars are just another great idea to use a Cricut cutting device. A calendar is filled with 12 months. You may get creative and hunt for designs on your cartridge or software that may reflect the whole month that's on your calendar. If we are in the month of December, you may seek out layouts which fit the mood and sense of December. Start searching for snowmen, reindeers, and Christmas trees. I promise you that you have got all the layouts you will ever want inside your applications or cartridge.

Remember, only your creativity can limit what you do. These Cricut jobs could possibly be used either for personal satisfaction or revenue generating purposes. Be creative with your preferred machine. You never know what kind of thoughts can pop into your mind.

This report clarifies the numerous uses of the Cricut Jukebox system, however, a justification for your Cricut system, called the private electronics monitoring system will be in order. The Cricut personal cutter is an entire cutting platform employed for crafting. It is lightweight and designed to help with your home, office or faculty scrapbooking and other jobs. It's fairly user friendly and exceptionally convenient. As a plug in, cut and design machine, it is completely beneficial for individuals focusing on card making, scrapbook construction and perhaps even paper crafting.

However, the Cricut cutter system needs cartridges to get the job done. It has lots of cartridges to cut layouts of any kind and any dimension, determined by the selection of the consumer. People can shell out a great deal of time loading and reloading individual cartridges they work with. To be in a position to make unique layouts and cut them out, you need to go from one cartridge to another, which might be quite time consuming. But there is a machine designed to lower the issue of loading and reloading, or changing of cartridges - voila! - the revolutionary Cricut Jukebox machine.

What's this Cricut Jukebox apparatus? It is an extremely valuable machine, valuable to anyone who participates in the art of crafting. Cricut Jukebox, which looks like a simple cartridge, isn't just a box. It is a system or tool that, when plugged into the Cricut cutter system, can supply six (6) cartridges of special layouts and measurements. Apparently, the wide variety of those 6 cartridges should be up to your liking and wants. This application will surely provide you a hand in your cutting and designing tasks. The Jukebox eases and eliminates the trouble of shifting the cartridges in and out of your Cricut machine.

There are more attributes of this machine you need to find out about. This Cricut Jukebox system is searchable. Which means you can operate with more than one jukebox whilst working with your Cricut machine. Considering the jukebox system gives a unique quality that enables three jukeboxes to be used at the same time, you've got the means of using more cartridges when you have the need to. One jukebox holds 6 cartridges, so therefore, in case you simultaneously use 3 jukeboxes in one time, you will have 18 cartridges prepared to use. How can that? Each Cricut jukebox is equipped with cable wires - a very simple procedure to follow. Just plug in one jukebox on your Cricut device and plug in a different jukebox to the first one which you attached into the primary Cricut apparatus, which you can then proceed to plug them one after another. In other words, connect one with a different one- easy!

Another fantastic feature of the Jukebox, is that you can stack them to minimize space in your office, allowing you to run them safely in minimal space - and far more, it provides a compartment where you might safely stack your own cartridges. The Cricut Jukebox is portable and simple to use, thus, you've got benefit as well as simplicity of use. It isn't necessary to depend on a person changing cartridges, as soon as you're in a position to take advantage of just pushing buttons, and keeping cartridges of your choice at the tip of your fingers!

Although, all the variations of Cricut cutting machines function in a similar technique to some extent using only a lot of variation to the specific same layout and attributes, the Cricut Design has emerged as a versatile system which has changed the crafting industry by introducing a couple of new features that improved its functionality.

The Cricut machine lets users cut many letters, shapes and words for classroom décor, signage, scrapbooks, and a whole lot more.

CHAPTER SEVEN

HOW TO CREATE PERSONALIZED PILLOWS

Among my favourite characteristics of Cricut Design Space is your capability to use system fonts. As a consequence, you may download fonts from the Web and use them in your regular crafting world! I really like it. Whenever you have the liberty to use any font you would like, the alternatives for typography projects explode!

For my initial typography job, I made a pillow with one of my own favourite quotations on it- "At the touch of love, everyone becomes a poet," by Plato.

There are a lot of sites where you can download fonts at no cost, but my favorite is dafont.com. Dafont.com permits users to upload fonts they've designed. Be aware that most of the fonts have special instructions and asks that you use them for individual use only.

Want to make this pillow? It is ready-to-make!

Materials needed:
Cricut Explorer® or Maker machine
Cricut® 12" x 12" standard grip mat
Cricut weeder tool
Purple iron-on
Gold iron-on

20" x 20" pillow shape and protect

Easy press or iron

Press fabric or clean cotton fabric

1: Download your favourite

The fonts you will need to make this job are: Mastoc, Bream Catcher, and Authentic Hilton. Click the hyperlinks to be taken to www.dafont.com.

****Please be aware that Mastoc and Authentic Hilton should be used for individual use only. ****

You have to download and install these fonts for the job to get the job done.

To install, start the downloaded font (tagged .ttf) and put in it to your PC.

It works better if you download the fonts prior to launching Cricut Design Space. Otherwise, you will want to close the browser and then reopen it after installing the fonts to automatically refresh your font file.

2: Produce design

Insert text on your canvas. The fonts will be automatically a part of this system fonts as soon as you've installed them. You can filter fonts in Design Space by clicking system fonts from the top window.

Once I have determined which words I need in each font, then I begin placing them in a design. The very first step would be to weld the script fonts collectively. Choose the words and ungroup the letters.

Transfer the letters next to each other before you are happy with how they look. Then pick each the letters and weld them together.

Organize all the words on your layout, pick all the words, and weld them together so that the words will cut as one whole design.

3: Cut out design

In Cricut Design Space, cut pictures from the iron-on. Make sure to check the "mirror pictures (for iron-on)" box in the mat preview before you cut. (if cutting numerous mats, make certain to check that box to get every mat which has iron-on.)

4: Put iron-on

Weed excess iron-on round the picture.

5: Use iron-on on pillow

Follow the program directions for Cricut iron-on to stick the cut phrases onto the front of the pillow.

Use our easypress or an iron on the purple picture first, then do the gold image.

Supplies you'll need:

Cricut Explore or maker machine

Cricut® 12" x 24" standard grip cutting mat

Cricut® tools, weeder

Cricut® iron-on lite in gray

Cricut® iron-on lite in black

Cricut® iron-on lite in red

Cricut® iron-on lite in cyan

Cricut® iron-on lite in maize

White canvas cloth

Red cotton cloth

Blue cotton cloth

Literary cotton cloth

Dark cotton cloth

Dark and white cotton cloth

Iron or easypress

Press fabric or clean cotton fabric

Scissors

Sewing machine and thread

Needle

Polyester fiberfill (not pictured)

1: Cut your pictures

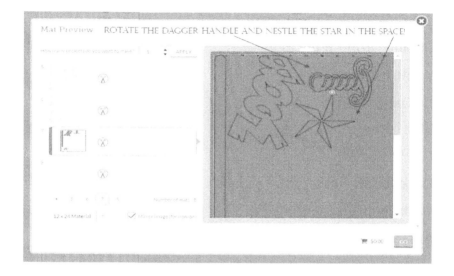

Open the pillow job in Cricut Design Space™ and click on create it. The project file contains the pictures for thirteen cushions: (two) swords, (1) dagger, (1) grenade, (3) ninja stars, (1)"flourish" term, (2) hitting fists, (1) bomb and (2) knives. Bear in mind that if you merely wish to cut some of the cushions or more of a single kind of cushion, you could always click on customize rather than make it and change the document to satisfy your requirements.

Some important tips for this job:

-Make certain to click on the "mirror picture (for iron-on)" button for each mat in the job on the mat preview display. Considering that every one of the mats includes iron-on, you'll have to click onto each mat and select to mirror the picture.

-The program determines where the cuts will happen on the mat. For this job, I needed to save my iron-on material, and so I moved the pictures around on the mat to make the best use of the leading area. Additionally, this is performed in the mat preview display.

-Simply click on each picture and move them around until they are tucked right into each other. This ninja star would not have cut since the iron-on substance is 19" long and the star was set lower than that on the mat.

-Assess each mat. I transferred pictures around on all them.

2: Iron images onto canvas

Iron the pictures onto white canvas leaving approximately 5-6" of distance between pictures for cutting and stitching. It is possible to accelerate the process using our easypress as it's a larger surface compared to a conventional iron and much more consistent heating throughout the plate.

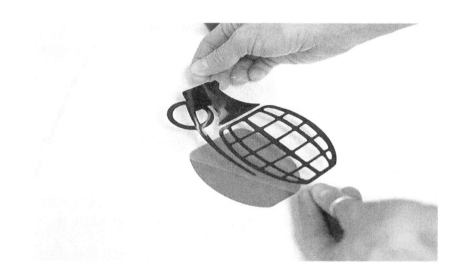

For the layered images, begin with ironing the base layer set up. Eliminate the liner.

Twist the top picture over the base image and iron in place. You can find more directions about the best way best to use Cricut® iron-on here.

3: Cut fabric shapes

Use scissors to cut each picture. Make sure to leave at least 2-3" of space around the pictures for stitching seam, trimming and cutting.

You do not need to be perfect! The attractiveness of these interesting cushions is their wonky shape that really adds to their appeal.

4: **Cut out sourcing**

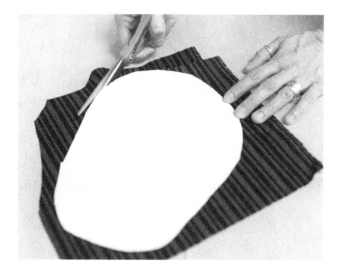

Set the cut canvas pictures face down on the backing cloth (right sides together). Use scissors to cut the backing to coordinate with the front part.

5: Stitch fabric together

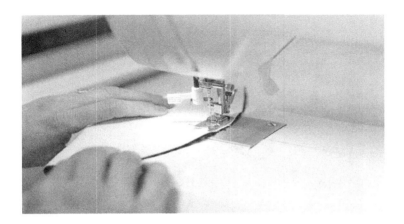

Use a sewing machine to sew around the borders of every cushion. Leave about two 1/2" open (unstitched) for turning and stuffing. I used 1/4" seams.

6: Switch pillows and materials

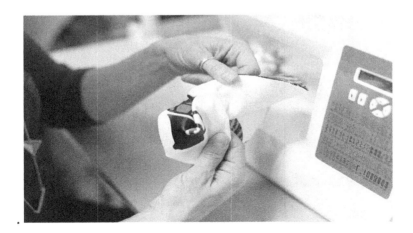

Turn the cushions inside out and stuff them with fiberfill.

7: Hand-stitch the openings

Use a needle and thread to hand-stitch the openings shut.

CHAPTER EIGHT

THE WAY TO MAKE PRSONALIZED TOTES AND DECORATIONS

In case you have tried painting or stencilling cloths, then you know it could be rather hard to obtain a quite clean and consistent outcome. Prepared to meet a new love?

Iron-on vinyl! Now I'm going to discuss with you the way to use Cricut iron-on vinyl along with the Cricut Easy press two to make a gorgeous floral canvas bag really fast and readily. Wouldn't this tote be a fantastic present for a friend who enjoys gardens and flowers? Oh, also do not forget your mother!

Step 1: Cut the Cricut iron-on vinyl

If you're just getting started on Cricut projects, assess outside this comprehensive Cricut beginner's tutorial about how I generated my very first Cricut job (a gorgeous card!) in only 20 minutes.

Significant: After launching the floral design in Cricut Design Space, resize it to match your job. Next, you'll be prompted to select materials. If you're using Cricut glitter iron on vinyl, be certain you click on the "browse all materials" tab to obtain the "glitter iron-on," since it's thicker to cut compared to the normal iron-on vinyl. (See picture below.)

Click "mirror picture (for iron-on)" accordingly as it flips your picture. This isn't too crucial here but it's great to form a custom for iron-on projects so once you produce something with numbers or letters, it is going to go on properly.

Put your iron vinyl glistening plastic-side down on your standard grip cutting mat. Insert the mat into the Cricut, press clip, and see the magic happen.

Do not peel off the Cricut vinyl sheet off the mat however. We will eliminate the excess vinyl that is part of your layout.

Use the Cricut weeding tool to prop up a tiny corner, then peel off the piece. This Cricut tools fundamental place is amazing: it comprises the weeder, scraper, and spatula that I love, and much more! As you go, you'll see a small bit of glitter staying on the sheet. This is no issue.

The weeding tool made the process so much simpler. As soon as you finish weeding, peel the plastic sheet using the plastic layout attached onto it. We're now prepared to iron it onto our canvas tote bag!

Step 2: Move vinyl layout onto clean canvas tote bag.

You can use an iron to do iron-on plastic jobs, but an iron may have very irregular temperatures in the center to the outer borders. The heating on the Cricut Easypress is totally across its surface just like a conventional heat press. It's super-fast to warm up and as simple to use as an iron.

Set the Cricut Easypress to 315°. It will heat up in about 2-3 minutes. Put the bag on an even surface like an ironing board. I used the Cricut Easypress mat that's created for using together with the Easypress heat press machine. The mat provides a smooth and even surface on front of the canvas bag, and is super simple to store when not being used.

Put the design together with the glistening plastic side on the canvas tote bag. The plastic protects the Cricut vinyl. Never allow the vinyl to touch the iron directly!

Put the layout in the specific place you need on the canvas bag and put the Easypress at the top for 30 minutes.

My layout is somewhat larger than the 9″x9″ region of the Easypress, therefore I transferred the Easypress to distinct locations and replicated the 30 second procedure.

Allow the vinyl to cool, and then peel the plastic back from your picture. Such an exciting moment!

The vinyl should adhere. If you discover it begins to pull up, put the vinyl down and use more heat on your area.

Our new canvas tote bag is ideal for all of the overflowing prosperity from our backyard!

PERSONALIZED HOME DÉCOR

The Cricut machine is an excellent tool. The world of scrapbooking hasn't been the exact same ever since the debut of the Cricut cutting machine. This instrument has revolutionized how we cut designs from paper, vinyl and cloth.

Back in the times of metal and wood, the craft of maintaining memories was crude. Man used nothing but paintings, portraits and writing as tools for capturing memories and making certain future generations could see them. There was not any way of recording voice and movement back then. As the years progressed, things changed.

Tech experienced a massive boom as a result of the fantastic minds that inhabited the late 18th and 19 century. You look around you and that which was once a dream is currently possible. A method or procedure that was introduced in the 19th century that was regarded as a distinctive method of preserving memories has been the method of scrapbooking. This procedure involved the introduction of a publication which would house images that shared a frequent theme.

When scrapbooking was comparatively fresh, things were hard as it came to the real process of producing them. The conceptualization was simple, but the cutting stage was what challenged scrapbookers far and close as the procedure alone demanded the most stable hands on Earth. However, with the debut of the Cricut cutting machine, the cutting-edge stage has been quite simple. There's really a whole lot of Cricut jobs out there which it is possible to participate in by means of your Cricut machine. Let us talk a little about a few of them, shall we?

You will find Cricut jobs which may enable you to attain personal satisfaction or assist you in making money. For many people the Cricut system is simply confined to simply being an instrument for scrapbooking. In fact, the Cricut cutting machine may be used for a whole lot of things. Keep in mind, the layouts which are observed on your applications tool or cartridges may be used for a great deal of things.

For starters, it is possible to make greeting cards. I am pretty much convinced that most people have had horrible experiences before which are connected without finding the ideal gift card. Using a Cricut machine and application or a cartridge, you may make your very own personalized gift cards. You may either sell them in case you would like to or simply continue making cards for your personal satisfaction.

You will find so many Cricut projects which you can participate in using all the Cricut machines. The rule of thumb would be to be imaginative and never allow your mind to set limitations.

CRICUT SUGGESTIONS FOR PROMOTING YOUR GREETING CARD PROJECTS

You've just bought a Cricut private cutting machine together with its collection of cartridges you can use to begin a wonderful job. This revolutionary machine has revolutionized the arts and crafts hobby all around the world. Using its popularity increasing, you also need to think of great Cricut tips which you can begin promoting in local craft displays, on the Internet or in the regional specialty shops near you.

To get started with your Cricut jobs, allow me to assist you with some good Cricut ideas that you can start with. With these terrific ideas, now you can produce your initial line-up of innovative craft layouts and individuals can search for your services or purchase your creations. Isn't it a superb idea to do what you really love and in precisely the exact same time earn a little excess money?

You can start your initial Cricut job by producing a range of cards. Be innovative and creative with your card undertaking. Come up with a number of greeting cards. Include birthday cards for many ages and sexes, a few thank you cards, anniversary, sympathy and blank cards for use for almost any events. Embellish you cards with blossoms or phrases adorned with unique shapes and colors produced from the Cricut cutting machine. You may pack them in sets up to 6 cards a box, as well as make customized envelopes t you may create using your system.

Bundle your created cards nicely for shops owners to become interested in selling your merchandise. It may be a very professional business person and not only a crafter attempting to sell your hobbies. Together with your Cricut system you can also produce your cards. Apart from promoting your greeting cards from craft shops, you can take orders for events like baby showers, baby christenings, birthday parties and a lot more.

There's a site named shop handmade at which you can sell your things. The best part is this website needs no monthly membership fee. Additionally, there are craft displays or trade fairs where you set up a booth to exhibit your crafted cards and collections.

Cricut includes a succession of cartridges you may use with topics for Christmas, Valentine's Day, Easter, Mother's Day or Father's Day. With these cartridges you can produce a lot of ideas for your greeting cards for each event.

Another card job you could do is to make custom made wedding favours, wedding shower and a lot more. From the Cricut solution series there's a cartridge known as wedding for all of the fantastic wedding motifs you may consider. The home accent cartridge includes amazing flowers and designs you may use for your wedding gown.

Your Cricut suggestions for promoting your craft layout are endless and the possibilities are infinite. The best part is that you can earn additional money while doing what you love best! Have fun with your endeavours!

Cricut suggestions for scrapbooking

Scrapbooking is the most recent craft craze. With the invention of digital cameras, picture albums are left behind. At this time, you have a much better way to maintain your photographs. With the improvement of technologies, Cricut suggestions for making scrapbooks are as simple as a touch of button. Cricut private cutter came up with the Cricut Expression as the reply to your scrapbooking needs. This permits you to create a number of the most intriguing and appealing contours to decorate your most straightforward paper craft projects.

The Cricut is a lightweight machine and could be carried anywhere like an arts and crafts celebration. After traveling, the machine includes a carrying case made for traveling and features padding, handle and wheels. With electric power and enthusiasm for scrapbooking, you may start creating exquisite crafts.

The Cricut looks like a photo printer that lets you to cut and design unique layouts to use on your scrapbooking projects. It has the capability to make several shapes and dimensions up to 24 inches. The Cricut will cut any paper such as card stock, vellum and chipboard.

The Cricut Expression machine is a fantastic tool which can help make your jobs enjoyable to perform. It's a simple to use cutting platform which does require a computer to operate. It cuts letters, shapes and phrases in little or large sizes. Not only does it cut paper goods, in addition, it can cut thin magnets along with some cloth and etch eyeglasses. This enhanced machine will be able to help you conserve paper and also make many copies of your chosen design or shape. It may definitely take your scrapbooking job to another level of different Cricut ideas.

It may cost you $350 to have a Cricut Expression machine should you purchase it from a retail shops. But you can buy a cheaper priced machine via the Web for as low as $150. Cricut cartridges may cost you around $80, but it is possible to discover online bargains under $30. Each cartridge has over 2,000 pictures you can use broadly.

Produce beautiful scrapbooks, greeting cards, calendars, posters, signage, house decor, teaching tools, company promotional products, and statements in only moments.

Using its multi-function capacity, crafters like you may turn your imaginative ideas into unique works of art. Together with the Cricut machine, it is possible to set you standing as a skilled crafter. Now you can unleash your initial creations for others to respect as well as buy.

Your great Cricut ideas could be made by the Cricut Expression machine. With its varied functions and the capacity to make myriad of jobs, investing in this Cricut system lets you express yourself and do what is important for you personally. Creative scrapbook ideas are now able to be turned into an art.

Five easy Cricut vinyl projects which you must try

Have you heard of Cricut plastic? If you have the personal electronic cutter the Circuit Expression die cut machine from Provocraft, then there's a great likelihood you know of it. But if you are like many crafters, then you might end up reluctant to use your device for cutting plastic, not understanding the numerous prospective jobs this useful product can create.

To get you started, here are five simple projects to attempt:

1. Wall lettering

Wall letters are likely among the most well-known applications for Cricut vinyl. Before die cuts, homeowners would need to employ an artist or muralist whenever they desired favourite phrases or get phrases hand painted on their own walls. Either that, or they'd need a great deal of patience and a reasonable amount of ability to perform it themselves. But plastic die cuts generate a similar appearance, with a fraction of the hassle and price.

2. Storage containers

Should you be a company freak (or for those who have ambitions to become one!), then you are going to love this thought. Cricut vinyl may be used to cut decorative tags, which could then be affixed to the exterior of assorted forms of storage containers. As an instance, consider your scrapbooking place. It's possible to sort out different ribbons, buttons, beads, and other embellishments that you use for your designs into different glass jars, then use your die cut machine to cut tags identifying the contents of each jar. The identical concept applies to a kid's playroom. It's possible to cut out words (or graphics - based on the age of your child), which you could then stick to your children's plastic storage containers and containers, to assist your child in keeping her or his toys sorted and keep the place clean.

3. Yard signs

Should you have something to sell or a company to market, then you might wish to think about using Cricut vinyl to make custom cheap yard signs. Want an example? Garage sale signs will look amazing if made using this procedure, and they'll really be fun to create! The same is true when you operate a house childcare center or other home-based small businesses. You may use vinyl to generate custom signs for your lawn to get the word out to prospective clients.

4. Vehicle signs

The good thing about vinyl is that it's very durable. This makes it ideal if you would like to produce your personal "bumper sticker" or other sign for your car or truck. It is possible to use these car decals as an enjoyable expression of your identity or to market your company. As mentioned previously in this guide, producing your own customized signs is a fantastic way to inexpensively market your business.

5. House numbers

So that visitors in addition to emergency personnel can find their houses, many people prefer to place their own sign on the outside of the property. This is still another project which it is possible to produce using Cricut vinyl.

Tags, bags, boxes, and much more Cricut cartridge - 7 tips you can use now

Go above and beyond and learn exactly how much it is possible to produce using the tags, bags, boxes, and much more Cricut cartridge- 7 tips you can use now. Hailed for its innovative design, flexibility and concentration on utility instead of mere ribbon, the tags, bags, boxes, and much more Cricut cartridge is a must-have thing for any do-it-yourself ace.

1. First things first, Explore every bit of the exceptionally diverse and flexible Cricut cartridge.

Shoppers who haven't yet undergone the gloriousness that's this cartridge might believe it's only a one-note cartridge for all those random occasions when you want tags, boxes, bags, and even more. To the contrary, this cartridge is made for these pragmatic applications, but also for all those random moments of absolute craftiness.

2. Make tags!

The cartridge features tags within a vast array of designs, shapes and dimensions. Users may pick and choose as they please. Make customized tags for everything in gifts, garage sales, auctions, keepsakes and mementos, title tags and much more with the support of this unique Cricut cartridge.

3. Make bags!

For all those unfamiliar with the tags, bags, boxes, and much more Cricut cartridge, users may select a bag and along with the

Cricut machine can cut it. The bag, however, isn't fully constructed. All it takes is the smallest bit of adhesive, coordination and voila- you have a bag. Bags vary from purse-type satchels to baskets to cosmetic bags.

4. Make boxes!

Boxes can be particularly helpful for present giving, including keepsakes and for compartmentalizing the remainder of your life. Box designs vary, but like the bags, they do need a little bit of folding and building after the whole piece is cut out.

5. Use the whole cartridge to throw a lavish party complete with party favours!

Ideas include expanding the tags to make personalized, casual invitations, together with the tags as title tags for guests, together with the bags to keep party favours and last but not least, using boxes to carry snacks, candy or individual products.

6. Get the advantage of the distinctive capabilities.

Particular features make it possible for users to choose the tags, boxes and bags template and put in their own spin on matters. These choices include: window, mirror, mirror/window, mirror/windows, shadow, and blackout imaginative capabilities. Personalize each product even more by adding your own personal touch and distinctive effect with these attributes.

7. Produce jobs for your children or for your inner child.

Organize and spend some time on jobs including personalized jewellery boxes, colourful crayon boxes, matching purses for children and their dolls or possibly a cake shaped box to get a piece of birthday cake to go.

Quick and easy handmade Easter greeting card suggestions

Are you currently on the lookout for some fast, simple and very affordable handmade Easter greeting card ideas? If this is so, I've got two greeting card layouts I would like to discuss with you now. This undertaking could be great to create with older kids, scouting troops, church youth groups, paper craft classes as well as college classes.

We left those cards with 10-14-year-old girls for them to give to their parents for Easter. After they were done making them, they were rather pleased with their creations. If you do not have a Cricut die cutting machine (used to cut the ovals and lettering) you can hand draw and then cut out different sized oval shapes and you can buy letter stickers in the regional arts and crafts shop. We used the Cricut George and basic shapes cartridge for all these endeavours.

Items needed:

4" by 5" blank cardstock note cards with envelopes

Various scrapbooking newspapers (hooks and prints)

Decorative edge scissors and normal edge scissors

Adhesives - glue dots, glue sticks and glue pens

Various colored scrapbooking fine tip pens and markers

*optional ink pads and Easter sentiments rubber stamps

For all these 2 layouts we used self-stick plastic scrapbooking net from mint green and 4 mm round self-stick purple rhinestones.

For card number one:

Cover the front of the card with pink scrapbooking paper which has been cut to match. Employing the Cricut set on the amount one size placing and using the Cricut Georges basic shapes cartridge we cut eight ovals from various colored papers. Using the identical cartridge turn your dial to the shadow option and cut four ovals (we used dark blue paper) as those will function as the foundation for the eggs.

With your glue stick, paste a bigger oval on top of each bigger oval to function as your Easter egg. Using decorative scissors, cut part the remaining smaller ovals into different widths. With a glue pencil, glue up the cut bits onto the eggs and then let dry. (approximately 5-10 minutes). If wanted. . .use different colored markers to include polka dots and squiggles for your own eggs to decorate them further. Applying glue dots, then attach each egg onto the greeting card close to the top and moving across the front. Using the Cricut Georges basic shapes cartridge place your dial into the number two dimensions setting. Cut the letters out of moderate blue scrapbooking paper. Cut a strip out of white scrapbooking paper which measures 2" by 5" in size and then glue it to some dark blue scrapbooking paper that's cut slightly bigger than your strip. We used decorative edge scissors to add interest to the design. Glue this strip on the lower half of the card. With a glue pen glue every letter onto the snowy foundation strip to define the word Easter. If wanted. . .use an ink pad and rubber stamp to stamp a belief inside or compose your own personal message.

For card number 2:

Cover the front of your card with pink scrapbooking newspaper. With a part of self-adhesive plastic mesh in a mint green colour, attach this to the centre front. Use blue self-stick letters (in this instance we spelled out the word Easter) and put people right over the net strip. Employing the Cricut die cutting machine and the Georges basic shapes cartridge, then cut two purple ovals on the 2 1/2 size placing and onto the shadow impact, cut one moderate blue oval on precisely the exact same setting. These 3 ovals will function as your foundation for those eggs.

Employing the exact same 2 1/2 size placing cut six to eight more ovals from different coloured scrapbooking papers. Glue these ovals on every one of the larger ovals which you cut out. Employing wavy border decorative scissors, cut a part the rest of the ovals. Use a glue pen or a glue stick and use those bits to decorate your egg foundations. Once done, use adhesive dots to attach your eggs in addition to the vinyl mesh strip. We chose to decorate the egg at the centre with small purple self-stick rhinestones to add decorative attention to it. With an ink pad and rubber stamp, stamp your opinion inside or handwrite your message.

There you have it.

Two fast and effortless handmade Easter themes for greeting cards which you may make with older kids or make them yourself. Happy crafting!

CONCLUSION

Cricut is your new a conclusion of personal digital cutting machines focusing on the maximum advantage of things for home decoration, scrap booking, paper trimming, card making, and much more. Whatever you might do with a Cricut is only limited by your own imagination. These machines include Cricut cartridges for easy use. The cartridges comprise numerous amazing built in templates for a variety of dimensions and applications. This gadget can also be quite straightforward to watch over. The designs can be chosen from the cartridge or may be custom made using the Cricut Design Studio to take originality to elevated heights - but a computer is vital for this particular function.

The Cricut bundle comprises these:

Cricut machines: These will function as tools which perform the die cutting owing to some creative designs.

Gypsy: This is in fact really the entire Cricut cartridge library in one go. It is a hand-held device that comprises the complete Cricut Design Studio - to ensure any time we'll need to produce a design the Gypsy is conveniently supplied.

Cricut design studio: It is the full-fledged app for producing just about any design on a Cricut cutter. All you'll need is a computer. Not only that, but may be used to easily explore, cut and design the entire cartridge library. The program also gives a decision to conserve the design to potential requirements. Assessing a Cricut design has never been easier!

Cuttlebug: It is the personal die cutting and embossing system. It features different sizes and styles such as paper-crafting, house decoration, house tasks, events, and faculty tasks. The program is created by leading artists that offers sharp die cuts every time. Cuttlebug also comprises professional exceptional embossing for connections with its different feel and measurements, making it an outstanding system.

Cricut cake: This is an optional tool used for producing designer confectioneries for sandwiches and cakes and other snacks, in almost no time.

An advanced version called the Cricut Expression could be used for sheets as large as 24" x 12," therefore fitting into a measurement, be it personal or professional. Not only that, but it features cartridges and advanced possibilities, like the adding of colors, printing, and much more, making it ideal for many jobs.

Cricut is the handicraft enthusiast's best buddy, or for anyone who'd love to design and create. It supplies over 250 distinct designs in many of sizes. The designs could be up to compared an inch or larger. The different cutting angles offer precision cutting - all of this together with templates that are attractive collectively with interlocking alphabets, provide lots to select from.

Now that you've got your own Cricut machine, why don't you start making great jobs like handmade greeting cards? Start selling them in local craft exhibits, online, or at specialty shops in town.

Now everybody can use a little additional money. Your first of many Cricut jobs will be to produce an assortment of about 10 to 12 cards. Be creative, you are going to find a good deal of ideas it is possible to take into account. Contained inside this variety you've got to get a couple greeting cards (make sure you make cards for women, men and also cards for children), make sure you include thank you, anniversary, get well and a sympathy card.

Some more tasks that you're in a place to make on your Cricut cutting machine is going to be to make blank inside note cards for nearly any purpose. You will have many card ideas such as blossoms that could be layered over the cover by way of a rhinestone centre, or maybe just the expression "hi" adorned with a couple unique shapes. You're ready to package them up in sets of 4-6 cards. With your Cricut cutting tool that does a variety of tasks with the push of a little button. All types of ideas will start flowing from your creative mind. You can also produce decorated boxes to place your cards into.

Now you need to take your Cricut jobs with lots of your suggestions and take them into a shop (florists, bakery, salons, along with small gift shops) and also talk to the proprietor. Have a look at the pricing available for each and every shop proprietor. Make sure you customize the price sheet with the name of the company that you're extremely likely to furnish them. You'll look like a very professional businessman instead of merely a crafter expecting to provide your personal card ideas.

Some owners may even permit you to leave your cards at their shop on consignment and merely keep a percentage when you sell them. (I have done consignment earlier at a local florist and at a luxurious nail salon additionally and really did great. What a great spot to display your Cricut cards compared to in a place that is 95 percent women, who would be the very best shoppers. Besides the cards that I provided in these shops, I got special buys for baby showers and birth announcements) just be sure that you leave your business cards at these shops.

Clients might wish to get you for specific orders. It's likewise possible to market online at a wonderful location on the Internet called shop handmade, it's great since it's free. Or it's also possible to advertise your Cricut tasks at local craft displays. While creating your cards remember Christmas as well as other big holidays which people send cards such as Christmas Day, Easter, Mother's Day, or Father's Day!

Another of many jobs it's very likely to create together with your Cricut cutting machine will be to create a custom baby shower or marriage or maybe wedding invitation. There are lots of ideas for these sorts of cards. You will encounter a great deal of Cricut cartridges that are made specifically for these jobs. In the Cricut choice collection there is a cartridge called wedding to get all those wonderful wedding contours it is possible to envision, and they have a home accent cartridge that has amazing swirly flowers and shapes it is also feasible to use for a wedding theme. In case you choose to proceed into the baby shower or birth announcement training course, you'll see fantastic cartridges such as New Arrival and soon to be printed A Youngster's Year.

Whichever path you require be certain that you create several samples in several distinct fashions. Take them to shows, go to wedding retreats in the region, bakeries, florists and baby boutiques. I can't stop thinking of ideas. I just had another one to find a superb job. See I told you that your ideas will start to stream after you start with your Cricut cutting device.

In the event you have any party centers for children's birthday parties locally it's extremely likely you could supply, customize and create goodie bags, and title tags. Show them samples of numerous topics which you've got (formed from the Cricut cartridges that you have). Maybe you will compose a catalogue to leave there so customers will be able to discover the choice that you'd love to supply them.

Cricut is a well-known manufacturer of equipment everywhere in the country. It is an exciting and one of a kind gadget used by most women and guys who would like to do exceptional and innovative jobs. At this moment, there are just three different versions of Cricut: the Cricut Create machine, the luxury Cricut Expression and of course, the standard Cricut personal electronic cutter machine.

Before improving on how Cricut can raise the society, let's have a peek at its start. Cricut was initially made using a massive firm called Provocraft which was a tiny store. Approximately forty years before, the company of Provocraft started as a retail store in the tiny town of Provo, Utah. With their resourcefulness and creativity, the company eventually grew over the years. They finally had a total of ten stores with an approximately 200,000 feet distribution centre.

If you examine the standard Cricut machine, it looks like an inkjet printer. But it doesn't need a computer to be used at all. An ordinary person has the capacity to use its function since you do not need programming skills too. Among with its advantages includes being lightweight. Its blade even cuts thin and thick papers that vary from one inch to 5.5 inches in size.

Cricut just weighs a half lb and this includes the power connector. What's more, it's extremely easy to take it any place like parties or event demonstrations since it's a portable product. Using its distinctive and sleek design, it's suitable for almost any crafting workplace.

As stated earlier, it may cut to 5.5 inches but that's just one attribute that it has. It cuts borders and names to around twenty-five inches, so therefore, making it an ideal match to a paper functioning with a dimension of 12 x 12 inches. Unlike other manufacturers, Cricut's most important facet is it has the capability to cut a great deal of things. Cricut can also cut a paper which has an extensive variety of roughly 0.5 mm thick. Luckily, Provocraft has supplied additional materials such as designer paper pads together with cardstock pads which may be used together with Cricut cartridges. In reality, these two different sorts of papers are made to match perfectly with Cricut.

If you ask many Cricut customers, then they'd undoubtedly say that the Cricut digital die cutter is the best one of the best cutters. This is only because Cricut cartridges have a massive set of choices with respect to fonts, colours, styles and designs, therefore, fostering the most level of imagination without the necessity of a PC.

If you don't know, using Cricut cartridges can produce miniature folds which you set inside the Cricut for you to set the form of shape, layout, font or layout that you would like to cut on. The cartridge has distinct types. It includes: ribbon cartridges, licensed cartridges, kind cartridges, choices cartridges and classmate cartridges.

In the end, you are very lucky since buying a Cricut cutter also enables one to get a free cartridge! This totally free cartridge includes several basic shapes that might now provide you with the opportunity to create a few decorations and shapes. Otherwise joyful, you can purchase additional Cricut cartridges to add to your collection. The more cartridges you have, the increased likelihood of creating exceptional artwork.

Generally speaking, serious scrapbookers invest a great deal of money in their hobby. But there are numerous frugal scrapbooking ideas that could readily be integrated into your endeavours and designs to help cut down those expenses.

Standard household products, and yes, even things which would ordinarily end up in the garbage, can be used. Listed below are a couple suggestions that will save cash in your pocketbook, in addition to help you recycle items which would otherwise wind up in the landfill.

1. Cereal boxes

Should you possess a die cut machine capable of cutting chipboard, like the Cricut Expression, do not buy chipboard in the craft shop. Rather, use cereal boxes. When you stick vibrant paper into the cereal box die cuts, nobody could possibly guess it came out of your pantry! You might even use inexpensive cookie cutters as designs for your cereal box chipboard shapes.

2. Wallpaper remnants

Many wallpaper remnants are as amazing as the expensive papers in the scrapbooking shops. Paint and wallcovering stores normally have a library of background sample books. After the background is stopped, these novels are lost. Ask the employees if they'd give the publications to you rather than throwing them out. Regrettably, there's a great possibility that these samples aren't acid-free. Even though they might not be acceptable for your scrapbook pages, they're the perfect touch for handmade cards and other paper crafting projects.

3. Gift wrap

Think of all the gorgeous gift wrap that winds up in the landfill. Rather than throwing it away, recycle it. At birthday parties and other special events, consult with the guest of honour to learn whether or not she has some plans to use the gift wrapping after unwrapping gifts. Should they intend to throw it away, then you can amass a fantastic range of gift-wrapping paper which may be used for your own chosen paper crafting projects.

4. Fabric and ribbon scraps

If sewing is just another one of your hobbies, you know that cloth and ribbon bits are the ideal match for your paper crafting projects. A number of these cloth and decoration scraps are too little for stitching, yet will be the ideal size for accenting handmade cards and much more. Request your family and friends that sew to keep a Ziploc to accumulate their bits. Rather than throwing them out they could give them to you!

5. Office goods

Lots of the goods in the scrapbooking aisle are just adorned office equipment. Office goods, however, are substantially more economical, and may be jazzed up with hardly any work. By way of instance, paper attachments are essentially the exact same thing as the vibrant braids which are used for scrapbooking. Paint them with cheap acrylic paints to coincide with your designs.

Using a little creativity and innovative thinking, you're surely going to find even more prevalent household products which you can use for frugal scrapbooking ideas. Keep an inexpensive container useful nearby, and because you run across odds and ends that may find another life in one of your endeavours, put it in the container before you find a use for it.

Made in the USA
Las Vegas, NV
03 March 2024